A Comprehensive Journey into Ayurvedic Healing

Discover Balance, Healing, and Wellbeing through the Art of Ayurveda, Transform Your Life Through Ancient Indian Healing Wisdom

Dr. EMILY L. LAD &
Prof. VASANT GLASER

Dr. Emily L. Lad

A Comprehensive Journey into Ayurvedic Healing

Dr. Emily L. Lad

Table of Contents:

Dr. Emily L. Lad

Book Introduction

Ayurveda, the ancient Indian system of natural healing, has been a guiding light for countless individuals seeking balance, wellness, and a deeper connection to their innermost selves. This comprehensive journey into the world of Ayurveda invites you to embark on a transformative path, where ancient wisdom meets modern living, and where the key to lasting health and happiness lies within reach.

In the pages that follow, you will uncover the profound origins and rich history of Ayurveda, a tradition that has withstood the test of time and continues to offer invaluable insights into the intricate dance between body, mind, and spirit. At its core, Ayurveda is a science of life, a holistic approach that recognizes the inherent interconnectedness of all aspects of our being.

This book will guide you through the fundamental principles of Ayurveda, unveiling the concept of the doshas – the dynamic forces that govern our physical, mental, and emotional well-being. You will learn to identify your unique doshic makeup and discover practical strategies to achieve and maintain a state of optimal balance, empowering you to take charge of your health and embrace a life of vitality and harmony.

The Ayurvedic diet is a cornerstone of this ancient wisdom, and you will explore the art of eating for balance. Discover the power of seasonal eating, the healing properties of herbs and spices, and the profound benefits of fasting and detoxification. Embark on a culinary journey that not only nourishes your body but also awakens your senses and ignites your connection to the natural world.

As you delve deeper into the Ayurvedic way of life, you will encounter the transformative power of daily and seasonal routines. Establish a healthy dinacharya (daily routine) and embrace the wisdom of ritucharya (seasonal routine), cultivating a rhythm that harmonizes with the ever-changing cycles of nature. Explore the purifying power of Panchakarma, a revered cleansing process that has the potential to reset and rejuvenate your entire being.

Ayurveda is not merely a system of healing but a holistic way of living that encompasses every aspect of your existence. Discover the art of Ayurvedic herbalism and pharmacology, unlocking the potent healing properties of plants and time-honored formulas. Explore the profound connection between Yoga, meditation, and Ayurveda, and learn how these ancient practices can support your journey towards greater equilibrium and self-awareness.

This book will also guide you through Ayurvedic approaches to common ailments, providing you with a wealth of natural remedies and practical strategies to address a wide range of concerns, from digestive issues to pain management, anxiety, and insomnia. Delve into the realm of clinical Ayurveda and gain insights into the diagnostic methods and treatment programs that can be tailored to address more complex health challenges.

Ayurveda recognizes the inextricable link between mind and body, and this book will illuminate the profound wisdom of Ayurvedic psychology. Explore techniques to calm the restless Vata mind, cool the fiery Pitta emotions, and stimulate the stagnant Kapha spirit. Embark on a journey of self-discovery, where you will learn to embrace bliss therapy, spiritual approaches, and the healing power of emotional awareness.

Throughout this comprehensive exploration, you will be guided to bring Ayurveda into your daily life, creating a nurturing home environment that reflects the principles of this ancient tradition. Discover practical strategies for incorporating Ayurveda into family life, caring for elders, and even introducing these timeless teachings to children, ensuring that the wisdom of Ayurveda is passed on to future generations.

Ultimately, this book is a testament to the transformative power of Ayurveda – a living tradition that has the potential to shift your perspective, awaken your senses, and cultivate a deeper connection to the rhythms of nature and the profound wisdom that resides within you. Embark on this journey with an open heart and mind, and you will discover that Ayurveda is not merely a system of healing but a way of life that can profoundly enrich your existence, imbuing each moment with the essence of balance, healing, and profound well-being.

Chapter 1

Introduction to Ayurveda: The Science of Life

1.1 Origins and History of Ayurveda

Ayurveda is an ancient holistic healing system that originated in India over 3,000 years ago. Considered one of the world's oldest medical systems, Ayurveda has evolved over millennia into a sophisticated science of health and wellbeing. Unlike modern medicine which focuses on treating symptoms and diseases, Ayurveda provides a complete mind-body approach to prevention and healthy living.

The beginnings of Ayurveda are rooted in ancient Vedic culture. The primitive origins likely emerged from everyday observations of nature, the elements, and nutrition. Early shamans and healers slowly developed a practical and philosophical understanding of health through direct experience and spiritual insight. By the time early recorded texts appeared around 1500 BCE in the Atharvaveda and Rigveda, an extensive knowledge of preventative medicine and holistic therapies had already developed.

According to traditional accounts, Ayurveda as a formalized system of medicine originated with the divine revelation of the ancient Hindu scriptures known as the Vedas. The oldest and most foundational Vedas were said to have been passed down directly from the gods to sages and seers in deep states of meditation. These enlightened masters then transmitted this divine knowledge in spoken tradition for centuries before scriptural texts emerged.

The Vedas contain four books of knowledge – Rigveda, Yajurveda, Atharvaveda, and Samaveda. While the first three Vedas focus on philosophy, rituals, and incantations, the fourth and most recent Veda features detailed information on healing and medicine. Known as Rigveda or the ""Science of Life"", it describes principles of health, anatomy, diagnosis, medica plants, prevention, and treatment protocols that form the foundation of Ayurvedic practice.

Building upon the Vedas, enlightened sages compiled their wisdom into the earliest comprehensive Ayurvedic textbooks around 1500-1200 BCE called the Samhitas. Of these, only three major Samhitas have survived until today and are still used as reference texts. The most renowned is the Charaka Samhita, compiled by the sage Charaka over various editions. This extensive manual covers anatomy, physiology, diagnosis, pharmacology, procedures, prevention, holistic therapies, and medical ethics.

The Sushruta Samhita, compiled in several stages by the sage Sushruta, focuses more extensively on surgery, detailing surgical instruments and operations for numerous conditions. The third major classic text is the Ashtanga Hridaya Samhita from sage Vagbhata, which provides a concise compilation of the other two Samhitas in a more accessible form. These three foundational treatises are like ancient encyclopedias of Ayurvedic knowledge.

After the Vedic period, Ayurveda flourished as a respected medical tradition in ancient India. Legendary Buddhist monarch Ashoka helped promote Ayurveda across his empire in the 3rd century BCE. Major Ayurvedic learning centers and hospitals emerged at revered universities such as those at Banaras, Nalanda, and Taxila. Students came from far and wide to study this sophisticated science. By the medieval period, Ayurveda was ingrained in Indian society with hundreds of thousands of practitioners across the subcontinent.

Scholars and physicians continued to expand upon the classical texts over the centuries, authoring their own ""Samhitas"" with new insights and innovations. Famous works on Ayurvedic psychiatry, toxicology, fertility, and surgery emerged during the medieval period. As other medical traditions developed in other lands, Ayurveda incorporated outside influences into its growing knowledge base. It remained the dominant system of healthcare in India through the modern era.

With the onset of British rule in the 19th century, Ayurveda suffered a period of decline under colonization. Western medicine gained favor and funding, while Ayurveda was suppressed by the foreign regime. However, in the decades after India's independence, major revitalization efforts brought Ayurveda back into the mainstream. It continues to thrive as an important part of India's medical system today, with designated Ayurvedic hospitals, universities, pharmacies, and extensive research on integrating modern medicine.

Now appreciated worldwide for its natural healing approach, Ayurveda has come full circle with renewed global interest. As we struggle with the limitations of modern healthcare, this ancient wisdom offers profound solutions and insights that are arguably more relevant than ever before. By studying its history and timeless principles, we gain a precious resource to reclaim holistic wellbeing in today's world.The arrival of the Europeans brought major changes for Ayurveda and traditional Indian medicine. As Britain colonized the subcontinent in the 18th and 19th centuries, Western medicine gained increasing influence. The British regime promoted their own modern medical system and began to suppress Ayurveda through policies meant to solidify control.

Funding and infrastructure for Ayurvedic hospitals and colleges were cut drastically. Traditional medical practitioners were marginalized while modern medicine was encouraged. Western anatomy and physiology were imposed onto the Ayurvedic curriculum in government colleges, diluting classical teachings. To practice legally, Ayurvedic vaidyas were forced to comply with British medical standards and education requirements.

Threatened with extinction, Ayurveda entered a period of stagnation and decline. With limited ability to formally train students, many traditional Ayurvedic families had to close down their long-running practices. Ancient manuscripts were lost and classical formulas forgotten. The British strategy to sideline Ayurveda and promote their own medicine was unfortunately quite successful.

By the early 20th century, Ayurveda had faded from mainstream prominence. Modern medicine dominated India's health system, especially in urban areas. Yet in rural villages, many traditional vaidyas continued to quietly practice and pass down ancestral wisdom. Home remedies and Ayurvedic pharmacies also remained popular treatment options for the general public.

After India gained independence in 1947, the new government sought to recover and rehabilitate the nation's traditional systems of medicine. The Ministry of Health established departments for Ayurveda as well as other traditional practices like Siddha, Unani and Yoga. Educational infrastructure was rebuilt with new Ayurvedic colleges and hospitals under government assistance.

To help recover lost classical knowledge, the Institute for Post-Graduate Training and Research in Ayurveda was founded to do translations, research, and publications. Major initiatives were undertaken by both the government and private institutions to preserve ancient texts and revive Ayurvedic theory and training curriculums based on traditional standards.

Over the past few decades, Ayurveda has blossomed again as great effort has been made to reclaim its rightful place in Indian society. Today it stands recognized alongside modern medicine as one of India's officially sanctioned medical systems. Thousands of Ayurvedic treatment centers and registered practitioners provide services across the country. Nearly 500,000 Ayurvedic doctors have graduated from state-approved educational programs. Extensive scientific investigation and integration with modern healthcare continues to grow.

In fact, India is now experiencing a major Ayurvedic renaissance. There has been a concerted movement to thoroughly modernize Ayurveda and put it on par with Western medicine. India's prestigious All India Institute of Ayurveda, founded in 2010, spearheads advanced research on standardization, quality control, pharmacological analysis, and integration with conventional treatment modalities.

A Comprehensive Journey into Ayurvedic Healing

Cutting-edge studies are underway in genomics, nanotechnology, cancer treatments, microbiology, drug discovery and more. The Indian government has dedicated over $250 million dollars to expand Ayurvedic infrastructure and bring Ayurvedic hospitals up to the highest technological standards. India is determined to reclaim its medicinal heritage and offer Ayurveda's natural healing solutions to meet 21st century chronic disease challenges.

Beyond India, interest in Ayurveda has exploded worldwide over the past couple decades. As modern medicine struggles with limited symptomatic treatments for complex chronic illnesses, people are seeking out alternatives like Ayurveda that offer broader and more holistic solutions. Its comprehensive Knowledge of prevention, wellness and mind-body health fills major gaps in the current medical paradigm.

In Western nations, Ayurveda was largely unheard of until the 1980s and 90s. Then, as Eastern spiritual teachings helped spawn the New Age movement, yoga and meditation surged in popularity. This opened the door for other pillars of Indian wisdom to take hold internationally.

Pop culture exposure through celebrities like The Beatles and Oprah Winfrey helped spark curiosity. As more Americans and Europeans sought Ayurvedic treatment at wellness centers in India, they started demanding services closer to home. Today, Ayurveda is booming worldwide with spas, clinics, training programs, supplements and therapies offered across North America, Europe, and beyond.

However, serious challenges face Ayurveda's potential growth outside India. Few quality benchmarks or accreditation standards exist for practitioners or products in Western nations. Issues around cultural appropriation also arise as aspects of this traditional system are decontextualized or commercialized. Nevertheless, dedicated efforts are underway to nurture Ayurveda's spread globally in ethical and substantiated ways.

The future of Ayurveda is brighter than ever as we enter this new era of expanded awareness and skyrocketing demand. After being suppressed for decades under colonization, India is reclaiming and reinventing its ancient healing heritage with pride. And the world is catching on, hungry for Ayurveda's profound natural solutions to health and inner balance. If nurtured respectfully, Ayurveda could blossom into a truly global system benefitting all of humanity.

1.2 Core Principles of Ayurveda

At the heart of Ayurveda is a profound understanding of the natural laws and interconnected systems that govern all life. This ancient science observes the macrocosm of seasonal cycles and environmental energies as well as the microcosm of our unique personal constitution. By aligning ourselves with these natural rhythms, we can optimize health and wellbeing.

Several key philosophies provide the foundation for Ayurvedic practice. First is the concept that all matter in the universe consists of five basic elements - ether, air, fire, water and earth. These building blocks combine to form three life forces or doshas known as Vata, Pitta and Kapha. Each dosha has specific qualities and functions in the body and mind. Individual health depends on the balanced coordination of the three doshas within one's unique constitution.

Ayurveda also teaches that living systems are sustained by prana, a subtle energy which permeates all existence. The flow of prana is influenced by the three doshas. Imbalanced doshas disrupt prana, creating disharmony and disease. Restoring dosha balance enhances the vital flow of prana for robust health at all levels of our being.

A Comprehensive Journey into Ayurvedic Healing

According to Ayurveda, the universe is composed of interconnected dynamic forces that affect our individual existence. We are microcosms within the macrocosm. Therefore, outer ecology and environment shape our inner ecology and wellbeing. Through lifestyle in harmony with nature's rhythms, we sustain health and wholeness.

The concept of individual constitution, known as Prakruti, is another central principle. Based on the unique combination of Vata, Pitta and Kapha doshas formed at conception, Prakruti describes one's inborn physical, mental and emotional traits. Understanding Prakruti allows customized recommendations for optimal health through alignment with personal attributes and needs.

In contrast to Prakruti is one's current imbalanced condition called Vikruti, which manifests as disease or dysfunction. Ayurveda aims to shift Vikruti back towards Prakruti for each unique individual. Pathways of natural healing are chosen according to constitutional strengths and vulnerabilities. Wholistic approaches harmonize body, mind and spirit.

A complete Ayurvedic assessment also analyzes mental and emotional attributes, along with dietary habits, daily routines and life history. The entirety of one's lifestyle and experiences shape wellbeing. Therefore, sustainable healing integrates all facets of an individual's existence with their natural constitution and environment.

The central goal of Ayurveda is maintaining balance of the doshas to prevent disease and sustain wellness. Key preventative strategies include: proper diet and nutrition according to constitution and season; daily and seasonal regimens aligned with nature's rhythms; positive lifestyle habits that foster mental and emotional harmony; rejuvenating treatments to cleanse accumulated toxins and imbalances.

When imbalance inevitably arises, Ayurveda offers therapeutic measures specific to each doshic disorder. Herbs, diet, manipulative treatments, detoxification, yoga, and other natural modalities gently guide mind and body back towards equilibrium. The same wholistic protocols both prevent and relieve health issues.

In the Ayurvedic worldview, optimal health derives from living joyfully and virtuously, perceiving oneself as interconnected with all of nature. Disharmony manifests when we lose this big picture perspective. Cultivating higher qualities of compassion, gratitude, presence, and wisdom protects our vital balance.

Ayurveda is inherently individualized, holistic, natural and spiritual. As a medical science, it employs rational principles and modalities. Yet its perspective remains profoundly conscious of human life's ultimate purpose - fulfillment of the soul through truth and enlightenment. For the complete blossoming of our humanity into divine potential, Ayurveda gently fosters profound inner evolution.

While modern medicine revolves around surgery and medications, Ayurveda offers innumerable pathways of natural healing aligned with each person's unique makeup. Some of the major preventative and therapeutic modalities include:

Constitutionally customized diet, nutrition and lifestyle regimens based on the ancient wisdom of food as medicine and the cycles of nature. Using diet to gently pacify or stimulate the doshas is a cornerstone of Ayurveda.

Herbal remedies, plant extracts and mineral compounds tailored to rebalance each doshic type and health condition while being safe and effective. Ayurvedic herbalism is among the most sophisticated natural pharmacologies in the world.

A Comprehensive Journey into Ayurvedic Healing

Subtle energy therapies ranging from acupuncture and marma point massage to color/gem light therapy. These modalities regulate the vital flow of prana and induce deep systemic harmony.

Yoga asanas, pranayama breathing techniques and meditation to optimize energy channels and promote integrity of body, mind and spirit. The yogic arts are integral to Ayurveda.

Panchakarma purification programs involving herbalized oil massages, heat therapy, therapeutic vomiting, enemas, nasal cleansing and other detoxification methods to eliminate deep-seated dosha imbalances and toxins. Panchakarma is a crown jewel of Ayurveda essential for periodic cleansing.

The endless holistic therapies of Ayurveda synergize to restore inner balance in alignment with Prakruti. With time-tested wisdom refined over millennia, Ayurveda provides the most sophisticated system of natural healing ever developed by humanity.While sophisticated in theory, Ayurveda remains highly practical and down-to-earth. Recommendations derive from astute observation of how natural laws shape human life. By optimizing daily lifestyle factors, illness can be prevented, vitality sustained and inner growth cultivated.

Ayurveda provides personal empowerment for self-healing based on nature's wisdom. Through understanding one's unique mind-body makeup and how to harmonize with nature's rhythms, we gain tools to profoundly influence our health. Simple yet profound tweaks to diet, daily routines, herbs, and more can create radical wellness transformations.

A hallmark of Ayurveda is its recognition that every individual has unique needs. Healing protocols are customized according to constitution, current imbalances, digestive power, age, stage of life and many other factors. Recommendations for one person may be ineffective or harmful for another of different Prakruti. A skilled Ayurvedic practitioner artfully assesses each case.

In contrast to allopathic medicine's "one-size-fits-all" approach, Ayurveda offers personalized roadmaps to cultivate optimal wellbeing. Profound healing wisdom reveals how to use nature's pharmacy and rhythms as precision healing instruments for each distinctive individual.

There are certain key areas of daily living where Ayurveda provides essential wisdom for healthy lifestyle design:

Diet and Nutrition - The foundational importance of proper food choices and eating habits aligned with constitution and seasons.

Daily and Seasonal Routines - Waking, sleeping, exercising and other routines coordinated with cycles of nature for smooth bodily functions and energy levels.

Preventative Care - Simple home therapies like oil massage and nasal irrigation to regularly cleanse toxins before they accumulate.

Herbal Pharmacy - Plant-based medicinals tailored to gently rebalance each dosha and health condition without side effects.

Body Purification - Panchakarma programs to deeply cleanse toxins and imbalance from tissues for rejuvenation.

Yoga and Meditation - Integrating physical, breathing and mental yogic practices to harmonize and integrate body, mind and prana.

By optimizing these core areas of daily life through Ayurveda's profound wisdom, we set ourselves on the path of lifelong balanced health and fulfillment.

A Comprehensive Journey into Ayurvedic Healing

Incorporating Ayurvedic principles does not require dramatic lifestyle overhaul for most people. Simple adjustments like eating warm cooked foods or going to bed earlier can make a major difference. Ayurveda offers many easy, practical enhancements for health.

Nor does Ayurveda necessarily reject all conventional medicine. When aligned with doshic dynamics and one's constitution, surgical interventions or pharmaceuticals may be appropriate. Integrative Ayurvedic practitioners discern when modern medicine can safely complement natural therapies.

Above all, Ayurveda empowers responsibility for our own wellbeing. Through expanding knowledge and applying its tenets, we gradually transform into our healthiest, most integrated state of balance. Aligning with the profound intelligence of nature induces greater harmony and vitality at every level of our existence.

While allopathic medicine revolves around diagnosing and treating abnormal pathology, Ayurveda focuses on maintaining the integrity of physiology and positive health. Imbalance naturally arises when we diverge from natural principles of living. Ayurveda's primary aim is guiding us back into alignment - physically, emotionally, and spiritually.

This ancient science recognizes how our beliefs, attitudes and state of consciousness shape our life experience. To wholly transform the roots of bodily disease, we must also nurture our highest mental and spiritual qualities. Ayurveda views existence through the lens of our divine eternal nature, gently reminding us of life's deeper purpose.

As a science of holistic living, Ayurveda offers wisdom that penetrates far beyond physical health. Its principles help us fulfill the highest possibilities of human life – meaningful service, rich relationships, inner peace. By improving how we nourish ourselves, flow through each day, and interact with the environment, Ayurveda improves everything we think, do, and feel.

While modern medicine often compartmentalizes the complexity of human physiology into isolated symptoms and specialized fields, Ayurveda maintains a continuous whole-systems perspective. All facets of lifestyle are seen as interconnected in shaping health, from thought patterns to sleeping position. This profound lens reveals how to heal root causes, not just control scattered symptoms.

The Ayurvedic approach empowers everyone to positively influence wellbeing through simple daily choices aligned with nature's intelligence. Gradually we cease being victims of poor health. Instead, we become confident masters of our destiny, navigating life's challenges with equilibrium and inner security. We engage the journey of vida - continuous growth into life's deepest meaning and highest human potential.

Ayurveda is not a panacea and does not promise perfection. However, it offers invaluable knowledge for self-healing, fulfillment and conscious living within the perpetual ups and downs of worldly existence. This ancient science hands us precious keys to unlock our most vibrant health possible in body, mind and spirit.

1.3 Benefits of Ayurvedic Lifestyle

The holistic principles and natural modalities of Ayurveda offer profound healing benefits with regular practice over time. Ayurvedic medicine is not about quick fixes, but gradually transforming all facets of lifestyle for optimal wellbeing. While results manifest at different paces for each individual, most people find improved health, vitality and inner balance from adopting Ayurvedic rituals.

A Comprehensive Journey into Ayurvedic Healing

Some of the key benefits of integrating Ayurvedic therapies and knowledge into daily life include:

Ayurvedic routines like oil massage, nasal irrigation, regular meals, yoga and meditation optimize immune function and cognitive ability. Herbal tonics called Rasayanas rejuvenate tissues and biological systems, enhancing resistance and resilience. With regular practice, people report fewer colds, allergies, and health complications.

Fatigue, lethargy and low energy often result from imbalanced doshas and clogged bodily channels. Ayurvedic therapies like Panchakarma detoxification, herbal tonics and yoga cleanse blockages and rekindle agni digestive fire. People find daily activities require less effort and feel enlivened overall.

The emphasis on relaxation, mindfulness, soothing herbs and establishing sattvic rhythms of nature helps calm the mind and nervous system. Counseling based on the Ayurvedic understanding of emotions also provides coping mechanisms keyed to one's constitution. Most people feel more tranquil and able to manage life's pressures.

Using spices like ginger, fenugreek and fennel along with probiotic foods improves digestion and absorption. Abhyanga oil massage before meals primes strong agni fire. Yoga asanas massage the intestines and stimulate daily elimination. Gas, bloating, constipation and diarrhea issues tend to resolve with Ayurvedic protocols.

Ayurvedic routine includes going to bed early in tune with natural cycles. Calming activities like oil massage before bed, warm milk with herbs, meditation and Vata-soothing yoga relax the nervous system. People commonly report drifting into deeper, more restful sleep and waking refreshed.

Herbs like boswellia and turmeric reduce inflammation and discomfort in joints and muscles without side effects. Custom herbal formulas target the root causes of each type of pain. Therapies like oil massage, heat application and yoga therapy enhance circulation and loosen tissues. People often reduce or eliminate chronic pain medications.

Counseling based on Ayurvedic psychology offers sound coping strategies aligned with your unique mind-body makeup to smooth out anxiety, anger, sadness and other negative emotions. Daily routines, yoga, pranayama and meditation also induce a calm, balanced, sattvic state of mind. Overall mood and outlook tends to brighten.

Ayurvedic guidance on optimal diet and eating habits tailored to one's constitution and current agni ignition prevents blood sugar swings and fat storage. Herbs enhance metabolism and circulation. Yoga builds muscle and stimulates fat burning. People shed excess pounds, maintain healthy BMI and feel fit.

Herbal formulas, internal oleation, lymphatic massage and detoxification cleanse deep tissues, removing toxins and impurities for clear, glowing skin. A diet of fresh, whole foods provides micronutrients and antioxidants for youthful skin and lustrous hair from within. External beauty enhancements use natural herbs, oils and treatments.

Rasayana rejuvenation therapies, yoga and herbs like amalaki and ashwagandha scavenge free radicals, boost collagen synthesis, nourish tissues and renew the mind. Regular practice preserves youthfulness and mental acuity into older age. Quality lifespan is extended as tissues retain their natural resilience and regeneration longer.

Rather than waiting for illness to strike, Ayurveda provides personalized guidance for pre-empting problems through daily routines, seasonal cleansings and constitutionally aligned diet and herbs. When followed diligently, Ayurvedic protocols maintain excellent homeostasis and reduce disease incidence throughout life.

Perhaps most profoundly, adopting an Ayurvedic lifestyle realigns us with the healing intelligence of nature. Returning to natural rhythms enhances vitality and wellbeing in body, mind and spirit. We function optimally as our evolution intended - not contending with the environment, but flowing in effortless harmony.

While Ayurveda does not pretend to cure every ill, its practices offer invaluable holistic knowledge for preserving health, prolonging vitality, improving daily quality of life, and revealing each person's unique path to wholeness. Through heeding its wisdom, we access our deepest healing potential.The holistic principles and natural modalities of Ayurveda offer profound healing benefits when incorporated into regular daily practice over months and years. Ayurvedic medicine is not about quick fixes or overnight transformations. It is about gradually integrating ancient rituals and wisdom into all facets of lifestyle to promote optimal lifelong wellbeing. While individual results manifest at different paces based on consistency and other factors, most people find improved energy, strength, digestion, mental clarity, resilience and inner balance from adopting Ayurvedic routines in a step-by-step sustainable way.

Some of the key benefits of an Ayurvedic lifestyle include enhanced immunity and resilience, since rituals like abhyanga oil massage, nasal irrigation, yoga, meditation and consumption of herbal tonics called rasayanas optimize immune function and cognitive ability. With time and regular practice, many people report experiencing fewer colds, allergies, and health complications from common viruses and bacteria. Energy and stamina also increase, as techniques like panchakarma cleansing, use of digestion-enhancing herbs and establishment of regular mealtimes rekindle agni digestive fire and clear obstructions in bodily channels that previously caused fatigue, lethargy and low energy.

Mental equanimity improves as well, since activities like meditation, breathwork, chanting of mantras and consumption of nervine herbs rich in calming properties help reduce anxiety, restlessness and overwhelm by balancing the nervous system and mind. Healthy digestion and elimination are supported through consumption of spices like ginger, fenugreek and fennel that stoke agni and improve absorption of nutrients. Abhyanga oil massage before meals primes strong fire, while certain yoga postures massage the intestines and stimulate daily elimination. With these protocols, issues like gas, bloating, constipation and diarrhea frequently resolve.

Sleep normalizes with the Ayurvedic routine of going to bed early, in tune with natural circadian cycles. Calming nighttime rituals like self-massage with herbalized oil, consumption of warm spiced milk, meditation and Vata-soothing yoga enable relaxation of the nervous system and slipping into deep, restful sleep. Most people report waking refreshed and energized. Natural pain relief comes from anti-inflammatory herbs like turmeric and boswellia that reduce swelling and discomfort without side effects. Therapies like massage, heat application and yoga therapy enhance circulation, loosen tight tissues and address the root causes of pain for each individual. With Ayurveda, people often reduce or eliminate dependence on pain medications.

These are just some of the tangible physical benefits that improve daily lived experience,but adopting Ayurveda also realigns us with nature's profound healing intelligence in a fundamental way. Returning to natural rhythms enhances vitality, clarity and wellbeing holistically. We start to function optimally as our bodies and minds are meant to, not contending with the environment but harmonizing effortlessly. This inner realignment sets the stage for profound evolution physically, emotionally and spiritually.

A Comprehensive Journey into Ayurvedic Healing

While Ayurveda does not pretend to cure every health issue, its regular practice strengthens the foundations for wellbeing and reveals each person's unique path for reaching their full healing potential. Through heeding its wisdom patiently and consistently over time, we access deep nourishment for body, mind and soul.

1.4 How Ayurveda Views Health and Wellbeing

Ayurveda takes a profoundly wholistic view of health and wellbeing, seeing the mind, body and spirit as interconnected parts of one whole system. This ancient science recognizes that true health depends on nurturing all facets of life in balanced integration and alignment. Ayurveda's model of vitality extends far beyond just physical fitness or freedom from disease.

At its core, Ayurveda sees each person as a unique embodiment of cosmic consciousness - pure creative intelligence incarnate in a physical form. Health is the free flow and fullest expression of that cosmic life force as embodied in each individual. Anything obstructing or limiting that progressive life flow results in discord that manifests as illness on physical, mental or emotional levels.

Therefore, supporting health requires addressing root causes of stagnation or blockage at subtle levels of our existence. Diet, lifestyle, environment, relationships and state of mind must all be brought into harmony to cultivate freedom and balance within all layers of life - gross to subtle.

Ayurveda views the physical body as a vehicle for growth of the indwelling sentient consciousness that animates it. The goal of Ayurvedic healing is to clear obstructions in both gross physical and subtle energetic channels so our embodied consciousness can flow, expand and express itself fully through all aspects of human life.

At the grossest level, health depends on proper functioning of tissues (dhatus), waste removal (malas), and metabolism (agni). Ayurveda optimizes these bodily processes through herbs, diet, detoxification and massage. At more subtle levels, health relies on unobstructed flow of prana through energy pathways called nadis which interconnect the entire mind-body matrix. Yoga, meditation and pranayama balance the doshas to keep nadis open.

Mental and emotional health requires sattva - clarity, balance and wisdom. Counseling, mantra, and lifestyle regimens develop sattvic refinement for clarity of perception, tranquility and higher awareness. When all levels align in synergistic flow, we experience the embodiment of health - progressive awakening into life's deepest meaning and purpose.

Therefore, Ayurveda employs a diverse toolkit encompassing diet, herbs, massage, detoxification, yoga, meditation, counseling, surgery, medication, music, mantra, astrology, gemology, spiritual practices and more. Each therapy plays an important role at different levels of care to restore wholistic balance.

For preventative maintenance, Ayurveda's primary focus is strengthening ojas, tejas and prana:

Ojas - The vital essence that confers strength, endurance, fertility and resilience. Ayurveda replenishes ojas through proper nutrition, rest, reducing sensory overload and rejuvenation therapies.

Tejas - Inner radiance related to health of bodily tissues and mental clarity. Tejas comes from pure, sattvic living and practices.

Prana - Subtle life force that animates all activity. Prana is enhanced through breathwork, yoga and balancing doshas.

A Comprehensive Journey into Ayurvedic Healing

When ojas, tejas and prana are robust, they confer protection, vitality and adaptation. People with strong reserves tolerate stressors and avoid illness. Just as effective healthcare sustains wellness before disease arises, Ayurveda maintains high ojas, tejas and prana for lifelong wellbeing.

Ayurveda also emphasizes upholding positive mental qualities like compassion, gratitude, presence, integrity, and equanimity. Our emotional state and outlook shape our reality and health. Imbalanced negative emotions lead to distorted perception and breakdown on mental, emotional and physical levels. Cultivating a sattvic mindset anchors the body in grace and elevates awareness to its highest potentials beyond fear, anxiety and anger.

The influence of consciousness on human life cannot be overstated. Ayurveda recognizes that full healing requires personal growth - consciously fostering our highest qualities and purpose. Every condition offers an opportunity for deeper wisdom, self-realization and enhanced vitality. When aligned with nature's intelligence within and without, we channel life's challenges into catalysts for awakening.

While modern medicine compartmentalizes health into isolated organ systems and symptoms, Ayurveda maintains a continuous whole-systems perspective. Diet, lifestyle, environment, relationships, emotions, and spirituality are seen as interconnected factors shaping wellbeing. No condition stands alone. Ayurveda's profound view identifies how to heal root causes, not just control scattered symptoms.

This holistic lens empowers individuals to positively influence health through lifestyle aligned with nature's wisdom. We transcend limiting roles as hapless victims of disease or circumstance. Health's highest state emerges when our multifaceted existence harmonizes with the omniscient laws of nature - our microcosm reflecting the macrocosm's primordial blueprint for life's unfolding.

Ayurveda guides us back into this profound alignment. Healing enables the spontaneous flourishing of embodied consciousness towards deepest fulfillment - progressive actualization of our potential. Every layer of life's fabric converges within pure sentient awareness, which Ayurveda ultimately seeks to liberate through its integrative modalities of alignment.

This awe-inspiring opportunity for human growth and realization makes Ayurveda far more than just a medical approach. Its diverse therapies synergize to create wholeness on every plane - physical, mental, emotional and spiritual. Experiencing life through this lens permanently elevates existence.While Ayurveda recognizes our infinite human potential, it also accepts imperfection as part of embodied life. Some degree of imbalance arises naturally, offering opportunities for learning and growth. Therefore, Ayurveda meets us wherever we are in any given moment, providing tools to cultivate greater health, awareness and inner freedom from that point forward.

Ayurveda understands the dynamics of cause and effect that shape reality. Our accumulated past actions, experiences, diet and lifestyle habits create present circumstances. By making choices aligned with natural law, we experience positive effects like health and vitality. Choices against nature promote negative outcomes like disease and discord.

Yet Ayurveda encourages self-compassion. Once we understand these causal forces, we can make awakened choices for future well being instead of blaming self or fate. Through accumulated actions born of wisdom, we gradually transform the roots of mind-body disharmony into blossoms of health and inner peace.

This growth process requires patience, dedication and perseverance. Ayurveda provides a lifelong pathway of evolution - not instant perfection. Courageously confronting our vulnerabilities and immaturities is part of the healing journey. With compassionate understanding of our human development, Ayurveda patiently empowers ever-increasing states of balance, awareness and energetic flow.

Ayurveda accepts that disease and discomfort often provide the most powerful motivation for learning and implementing health-promoting changes. Like the pressure of coal transforms into the brilliance of diamonds, Ayurveda understands how to channel life's inevitable trials into catalysts for healing breakthroughs and personal transformation.

This alchemical ability distinguishes Ayurveda's holistic paradigm from conventional medicine. Ayurveda recognizes our embodiment as a precious opportunity for growth. Even incurable conditions become gurus on the journey of self-realization, heightening awareness and uncovering inner wisdom. By aligning with nature's intelligence expansively through all circumstances, we actively participate in life's healing opportunity.

The Ayurvedic view sees all material creation as a manifestation of universal consciousness. Since our essential nature is that all-pervading consciousness, we hold the power to consciously evolve our embodiment - physically, mentally, emotionally and spiritually. As human beings, we can choose whether to align with healing higher consciousness or allow the undertow of instinctual lower consciousness to hold sway.

Ayurveda provides practices that elevate awareness and align all facets of life with grace, wisdom and natural law. As we journey towards health's highest state, Ayurveda also empowers acceptance and surrender. Effort engenders progress, while equanimity and trust allow nature's innate perfection to unfold through us. This holistic approach integrates human endeavor and cosmic becoming, propelling the soul's purpose through refined existence.

While the full majesty of our human potential may seem far away, Ayurveda charts a course to its realization. As we walk the path of Ayurveda through the terrain of everyday life, we clear blockages and ignite inner healing fires of transformation. With applied knowledge and action, we gradually unleash our birthright for the evolutionary embodiment of health and awareness.

This understanding ignites hope - through intention and practice, positive change will blossom. Yet Ayurveda also instills humility, as we realize the mysteries at work within each being and throughout nature's intelligent cosmos. We become caring participants and observers, not dictators, of life's healing unfoldment.

Ayurveda provides resources to actualize health within the human experience, while surrendering attachment to specific results. We simply align ourselves with the harmonizing flow of seasons, cycles and universal forces using Ayurveda's guidance. What unfolds within that space is nature's providence - opportunities for learning, service and higher states of embodied consciousness.

This holistic paradigm liberates and empowers. We release limiting identifications with health conditions and honor the sacred integrity of life's journey in each moment. Ayurveda accepts the totality of existence - the messy, chaotic, mundane and magical. All experiences offer teachings to deepen wisdom and compassion. We discover health not by reaching some perfect state, but by learning to flow with life's natural harmony.

1.5 Integrating Ayurveda into Modern Life

While Ayurveda is an ancient holistic system, its timeless wisdom remains powerfully relevant for improving health and wellbeing in the modern world. Ayurveda's principles align elegantly with our current understanding of physiology, biology and psychology from modern research. By skillfully integrating Ayurvedic approaches into contemporary evidence-based medicine and lifestyle, we gain access to profound tools for optimal wellness.

Many assume Ayurveda requires dramatic rejection of modern life. However, this misunderstands Ayurveda's insightful paradigm. We don't need to radically change everything or discard scientific knowledge. Skillful integration weaves Ayurveda's holistic wisdom into any lifestyle for positive enhancement. With discernment, we can incorporate appropriate Ayurvedic protocols into diet, daily rhythms, relationships, self-care practices and conventional medical treatments.

For instance, constitutional knowledge about our unique mind-body type brings immense value for customizing fitness regimens, nutrition plans and stress management in today's world. We can tailor our modern healthcare using Ayurveda's profound individualized approach instead of the "one-size-fits-all" paradigm. Tweaking digital routines, office environments and self-care rituals enhances wellbeing.

By honoring the enduring relevance of Ayurvedic principles alongside scientific progress, we access perennial wisdom supporting modern vitality. Some key areas where Ayurveda integrates beautifully into contemporary life include personalized lifestyle medicine, since Ayurveda provides tailored protocols for nutrition, movement, sleep, stress management and environment aligned with each individual's constitution and life circumstances, profoundly optimizing any modern healthcare plan. Natural remedies like herbal medicine, aromatherapy, massage and other drug-free therapies from Ayurveda offer safe, inexpensive self-care options before turning to pharmaceuticals when necessary. Mind-body health is also powerfully supported through meditation, yoga, breathing practices, counseling, mantra, and Ayurvedic psychology, which overcome limitations of solely biomedical models.

Wholistic disease prevention utilizes Ayurveda's wisdom to proactively cultivate wellness by understanding interconnected lifestyle root causes of illness before modern diagnostics detect abnormalities. Patient empowerment is fostered by promoting responsibility for one's own wellbeing through knowledge of self-healing practices, dietary wisdom and establishing sattvic daily rhythms aligned with nature.

As scientific research continues validating Ayurveda's approaches, skillful integration combats the reductionism and compartmentalization still plaguing parts of modern healthcare. Ayurveda reconnects us to profound holistic wisdom refined over centuries through meticulous observation, testing and clinical outcomes analysis. By honoring both complementary streams of knowledge, we gain the best of both worlds - the potency of natural healing traditions alongside continually emerging scientific breakthroughs.

Several important factors help facilitate fruitful integration of Ayurveda into contemporary settings, including quality evidence from rigorously researched clinical studies assessing physiological outcomes and mechanisms of action using modern scientific methods. Cultural humility enables respectful, nuanced understanding of Ayurveda's traditional origins and complex evolution when integrating into Western settings. A holistic foundation through having a strong basis in Ayurvedic fundamentals before merging with modern modalities allows for safe, appropriate application. Skillful training in comprehensively integrating Ayurveda and conventional medicine promotes optimal synergy rather than discordance. An openness to ongoing refinement through respectful knowledge exchange, while retaining Ayurveda's core integrity, enables evolution and progress.

As the global community reconnects with this profound healing tradition, we stand at an unprecedented edge of possibility for reinventing medicine in a more holistic direction. Ayurveda's wisdom offers critical missing pieces for nurturing wholistic wellbeing suited to

A Comprehensive Journey into Ayurvedic Healing

21st century lifestyles.Skillful integration of Ayurveda into modern wellness paradigms requires maintaining the integrity of Ayurvedic principles and therapies. Diluting or misrepresenting the traditional knowledge risks losing Ayurveda's profound power when merging into contemporary contexts.

Honoring the sophistication and intricacy of these ancient sciences is critical. For instance, proper application of Ayurvedic herbal formulas considers not just ingredient combinations but also harvesting, processing, timing and Compatibility with each person's constitution and condition. Compromising any step distorts the therapeutic effect.

Therefore, authentic Ayurvedic education and quality standards for products and services are paramount when integrating into today's healthcare ecosystems and regulations. Many in the West promote distorted versions of Ayurveda aligned with popular trends but disconnected from traditional knowledge. We must uplift those rigorously conveying Ayurveda's classical depth.

That said, Ayurveda has never been frozen in time. It evolved across eras as practitioners enhanced knowledge through ongoing observation, research, debate and outcomes analysis - much like modern medicine's peer review. Ayurveda expanded its surgical tools and pharmacopeia based on clinical evidence over centuries. This spirit of building upon a revered foundation through reasoned investigation remains relevant today.

Therefore, integration also requires discernment regarding which aspects of traditional methodology require preservation versus areas that could benefit from contemporary advances. For instance, modern hygienic surgical practices enhance Ayurvedic treatments without sacrificing core therapeutic knowledge. Updated extraction processes may improve medicinal potencies.

Ayurveda provides a holistic framework into which updated tools and technologies can integrate if aligned with foundational tenets. We must remain vigilant against fragmenting Ayurveda into disconnected commercialized parts rather than honouring its sophisticated totality shaped by centuries of empirical refinement.

Ayurveda's reemergence at this moment reflects a timely rediscovery of innate self-healing capabilities supported by natural ancient sciences. Beyond just combating disease, Ayurveda offers profound wisdom for optimization, prevention and personal growth using the body's natural intelligence. No pill or procedure can replicate Ayurveda's extensive lifelong guidance.

Therefore, reducing Ayurveda into an "alternative therapy," or mine for commodified interventions risks losing its true gift. Ayurveda fundamentally empowers people with knowledge for self-healing and actualizing our highest wellbeing in harmony with nature. This timeless wisdom enriches any integrative care model focused on sustainable vitality rather than isolated symptoms.

Our modern dualistic worldview separates body and mind, individual and nature, science and spirituality. Ayurveda seamlessly weaves together these fragmented aspects of human experience. While biomedical science pursues specialization and micro-reductionism, Ayurveda maintains holism and the integrity of living systems.

Truly honoring Ayurveda requires incorporating its expansive viewpoint. Seeing ourselves, health and the universe interdependently promotes the happiness, connection and inner freedom Ayurveda has cultivated for millennia. Therefore, integrative efforts must internalize this profound paradigm shift.

Ayurveda's resurgence comes when people are rediscovering holistic modalities for sustainable wellbeing. We crave reconnection to community, nature and our deepest human purpose. Integration will be most fruitful when uplifting these universal aspirations for health and fulfillment that Ayurveda embodies.

Our modern lifestyles desperately need Ayurveda's wisdom. Its foundational principles, diagnostic approach, and diverse healing modalities are extraordinarily valuable complements to conventional treatments. This integrative fusion empowers human flourishing through nature's profound intelligence."

1.6 The Future of Ayurveda

As global interest in Ayurveda accelerates, the future looks bright for reinventing health paradigms through this ancient wisdom. But optimizing Ayurveda's potential in the 21st century also requires navigating important challenges around integration, education, research, access and regulations.

While still in early stages, pioneering efforts are expanding to implement Ayurveda in ethical, safe and substantiated ways worldwide. The profound wholistic solutions this science offers are too valuable not to share judiciously with humanity needing its guidance.

Much energy is focused on building infrastructure for Ayurveda's growth beyond India, its ancestral home. Educational programs are evolving best methods for transmitting authentic knowledge while contextualizing for other cultures. Supporting grassroots community clinics increases access. Research agendas are delving into Ayurveda's underpinnings using modern scientific methods to enrich global integration.

An important foundation being strengthened is rigorous undergraduate and graduate academic programs for Ayurvedic education outside India. Despite surging interest, very few quality training options exist, resulting in substandard practitioners and services. To prevent dilution, accredited universities are developing curriculum standards and clinical apprenticeships that honor Ayurveda's complexity.

These clinician training pathways are expanding to encompass other allied health fields. Integrative programs for doctors, nurses, pharmacists and other practitioners build competency in Ayurvedic modalities to incorporate into conventional care safely. Modern research institutions are also training scientists to undertake specialized investigations on Ayurvedic treatments using methodology that captures its holistic lens.

While still relatively sparse, research on Ayurvedic approaches using randomized controlled trials, mechanistic studies, whole systems qualitative methods and other rigorous designs is growing. Much more work remains to be done, but early efforts are beginning to map Ayurvedic physiology and therapies from a biomedical perspective. This evidence base will facilitate global integration, while deepening our own understanding of human functioning.

Increased access and affordability are also important for Ayurveda's growth, especially in underserved communities. Most clinical services remain limited to India or expensive spa-like settings in the West, putting Ayurveda's therapies out of reach for many. But pioneering non-profits focused on inclusion and accessibility are emerging to shift this imbalance through innovative care delivery models.

Striking the right balance between widely sharing Ayurveda's wisdom versus risks of appropriation and commercialization remains an ongoing challenge. Skillful discernment is required to uplift the core principles from a place of respect, while adapting the application for contemporary settings. True integration will come through honoring Ayurveda's essence rather than diluting it into fragmented products and services.

A Comprehensive Journey into Ayurvedic Healing

Appropriate policy and regulatory shifts are crucial to facilitate mainstream adoption. Most nations lack risk-appropriate oversight models for traditional medicine. Campaigns by Ayurvedic professional groups are pursuing national regulation changes to enable qualified practice and ensure safety without excessive barriers. The World Health Organization has also taken steps to support traditional medicine inclusion.

India itself may experience growing pains as it evolves Ayurveda rapidly from its ancient roots into a global wellness legacy. Important debates are underway on how much innovation and modernization should be allowed versus preserving traditional knowledge. New institutes aim to reinvent Ayurveda using the latest biomedical tools, while traditionalists argue this distorts its wholistic foundation.

Skillful balancing is required to uphold Ayurveda's core wisdom grounded in nature while allowing carefully considered advancements. Ethics, sustainability and wisdom transmission must remain foundations amidst any modernization efforts. The full beauty of Ayurveda blossoms through harmonizing science and spirituality.

This renaissance is an open opportunity for collaborative synergy, not divisive dogma. Ayurveda's growth will be fueled by inclusive innovation networks, not proprietary ownership. The community must uphold respect, humility and service as guiding principles as Ayurveda spreads globally.

Despite complexities, by learning from past missteps and honorably conveying Ayurveda's sophistication, we can collectively steward its rightful place nourishing health in the modern and future world. If nurtured conscientiously, Ayurveda promises a profoundly hopeful paradigm shift toward wholistic wellbeing in the 21st century and beyond.Realizing Ayurveda's immense untapped potential in the 21st century requires acknowledging this ancient science's vulnerabilities. As global adoption accelerates, upholding Ayurveda's sophistication and preventing dilution will be critical priorities.

While modern tools and teaching methods are needed, safeguarding the heart of traditional knowledge transmission through long-term guru-shishya mentorship remains essential. Ayurveda's wisdom extends far beyond diagnostics and therapies into subtler dimensions of human existence only absorbed through experiential learning.

Retaining Ayurveda's wholistic foundation must be balanced with scientific evidence. Research needs to capture Ayurveda's complete picture, not just dissect isolated aspects. For instance, customizing interventions to each individual's constitution and imbalances is a core emphasis needing retention.

Preserving Sanskrit textual references and terminology also maintains fidelity, even when simplifying concepts for broad sharing. English cannot capture the nuanced essence of key Ayurvedic concepts which emerge from ancient Vedic philosophies.

Appropriate branding and marketing is another sensitive balance as Ayurveda emerges as a global wellness industry segment. Promoting life-affirming aspirations over playing on fears and insecurities will be important for upholding Ayurveda's sattvic essence.

For expanded access, cost reduction must be balanced with fair wages for skilled labor and high quality ingredients. Ayurveda's treatments take significant time and rare botanicals require sustainable scaling models. Digital tools may help with efficiencies but not fully substitute for human therapy.

Maintaining safety alongside growth will require diligent monitoring of side effects and contraindications, especially with new product formulations and integrative applications of therapies. Caution with drug interactions is critical as people combine Ayurveda with conventional medications.

Preserving ecological sustainability is also paramount as global demand scales production of Ayurvedic herbs and products. Overharvesting endangered botanicals like sandalwood already threatens sustainability. Conscientious stewarding of Ayurveda's natural resource foundations is vital.

The future of Ayurveda must honor its spiritual roots despite secular modern tendencies. Seeing ourselves as interconnected to nature and each other is foundational for Ayurveda's holistic paradigm. Uplifting these universal human values supports an enlightened trajectory.

Balance between tradition and innovation requires carefully discerning what core ancient wisdom to preserve intact versus areas appropriate for modernization. For example, certain dietary restrictions may be updated based on new nutritional knowledge.

Skillful integration will sustain Ayurveda's essence while adapting applications to different cultures. Discernment is required to avoid distortions like decontextualizing Ayurvedic therapies into spa-like services or religio-philosophical confusion.

Most importantly, upholding Ayurveda's transcendent vision for humanity remains imperative amidst any growth efforts. Beyond just physical health, Ayurveda illuminates the embodied spirit's purpose - liberation into eternal bliss consciousness. This enlightened understanding must steer Ayurveda's future.

Despite risks, global collaboration focused on ethically sharing Ayurveda's wisdom has monumental potential. This reawakening comes as humanity is rethinking health, environment, society and consciousness. If nurtured conscientiously, Ayurveda can help midwife a new era of harmonious living.

But first we must walk back from the brink of unsustainable imbalance. Applying Ayurveda's principles of prevention and holistic wellbeing is urgently needed to curb epidemics of modern chronic diseases. Ayurveda's knowledge offers real hope for those disillusioned with reductionist healthcare models.

The future of Ayurveda promises a profound paradigm shift toward holistic wellbeing globally. It offers living guidance into the right relationship between humans, nature and the cosmos essential for our times. May this auspicious wisdom tradition lead us into health, balance and spiritual awakening.

Chapter 2

Understanding the Doshas: Vata, Pitta, Kapha

2.1 Characteristics of Vata Dosha

In Ayurvedic philosophy, all matter and energy in the universe is composed of five basic elements - ether, air, fire, water and earth. These building blocks combine in different proportions to form three life forces or doshas known as Vata, Pitta and Kapha. Each dosha has distinct properties and functions within the body and mind.

Vata dosha is composed of ether and air elements. It governs all movement in the mind and body including circulation, respiration, nervous impulses and eliminative functions. Vata also controls the movements of Pitta and Kapha doshas. Imbalances in Vata often underlie imbalances in the other two doshas. The main properties of Vata dosha are dry, light, mobile and cold. Just as wind moves swiftly around the world, Vata provides the quick impulses that initiate all activity. Other common qualities of Vata include rough, erratic, dispersing and subtle. When Vata is balanced, the mind and body transpire gracefully. When Vata is excessive or disturbed, it leads to irregularities, anxiety and instability.

In the body, Vata governs muscle and tissue movement, breathing, blinking, cellular metabolism, heart rate and pulsations in the circulatory system. All sensory signals, nerve impulses, gland secretions and eliminations of urine, stool and sweat fall under Vata's domain. The mind relies on Vata for all thoughts, perception, creativity and expression. Vata resides mainly in the large intestine, pelvic cavity, thighs, skin, ears and bones. Imbalances often first appear in these areas through common Vata disorders like constipation, sciatica, dry skin and ringing in the ears.

Vata is the dominant dosha in childhood as the body and mind are developing. It naturally increases through old age as tissues become drier and less stable. Psychologically, Vata manifests as quick intellectual understanding, flexibility, creativity and changeability. When balanced, Vata brings energetic inspiration, lively imagination and keen sensitivity. However, excess Vata leads to fear, worry, racing thoughts, overactivity, forgetfulness, distraction and difficulty focusing.

People with prominent Vata characteristics often have a lean, thin build with prominent joints and limbs. They tend to have cool, dry skin and a darker complexion. Their hair is frequently fine and prone to dryness and split ends. Constipation is common and hunger and digestion tend to be irregular. Energetically they are highly energetic in short bursts but have difficulty persevering. Mentally, Vata types are very creative, inquisitive and restless.

Vata people are quick moving, enthusiastic explorers who learn and adapt readily but also stress easily. Light, cold, dry or erratic qualities in food, climate or lifestyle disturb Vata, while routine, warmth and moisture bring balance. Identifying Vata tendencies provides key insights for achieving health and harmony.When Vata is balanced, it promotes excellent communication between body and mind. All systems transpire rhythmically and effortlessly. Lightness brings energetic creativity, while mobility allows smooth flow and quick adaptation. Vata connects our awareness to sensory experiences and governs efficient eliminative functions.

However, when Vata becomes disturbed or excessive, numerous imbalances can manifest. Common Vata health issues include:

Anxiety, worry and racing thoughts
Insomnia and erratic sleep patterns
Bloating, gas and constipation
Excessive fatigue or hyperactivity
Aches, cramps and spasms in muscles
Tremors, tics and neurological issues
Forgetfulness and difficult concentration
Sensitivity to cold and intolerance of windy weather
Cracking joints, arthritis, osteoarthritis
Skin dryness and itching

Vata imbalances often relate to lifestyle factors that increase dryness, coldness, lightness or inconsistency. Insufficient hydration, warm meals or restful sleep can trigger elevated Vata. Excess travel, stimulation, change, fasting or physical exhaustion deplete Vata. Even enjoyable diversions like drinking or partying excessively derange Vata.

Maintaining regular daily and seasonal routines provides stability that balances mobile Vata. A calm, nurturing environment and sattvic lifestyle reduces Vata's anxiety and hyperactivity. Gentle yoga, meditation, oil massage and sleep hygiene smooth and soothe turbulent Vata. Moisture-rich foods cooked with warming spices ground restless Vata.

Beyond daily habits, constitutional Vata types need to skillfully manage activities that deplete their vulnerable elemental balance. High-intensity exercise, extreme sports, chronic dieting and overwork tend to disturb lightweight, mobile Vata - moderation is key. Travel is very drying and fatiguing for Vata types requiring extra rejuvenation. Stimulating sensory indulgences like loud concerts or horror films upset sensitive Vata.

A Comprehensive Journey into Ayurvedic Healing

When patterns of excessive stimulation or depletion override one's innate Vata limits, more serious mental and neurological issues can develop over time like insomnia, epilepsy, neuropathy, paralysis or nervous breakdown. Expert Ayurvedic guidance helps Vata types implement sustainability through appropriate diet, lifestyle and inner balance.

Vata imbalances also underlie many common seasonal health issues. As cold, dry qualities increase in the environment during fall and winter, they readily accumulate in those with predominant Vata constitutions. Radiant heat, hydration and oiliness provide essential antidotes to seasonal Vata aggravation.

One of Vata's most profound benefits is its role in the mind and consciousness. As initiator of all mental activity, Vata governs perception, creativity, cognition, intelligence and self-expression. When harmonized, Vata facilitates artistry, intuition, inspiration, insight and spirituality. However, Vata imbalances impair concentration, comprehension and inner stillness.

Therefore, balancing Vata is crucial for success in academics, profession, relationships and inner growth. Scattered Vata energy undermines learning, achievement and thoughtful communication. Calming excessive Vata through lifestyle alignment grants access to our deepest wisdom and creative potentials waiting beneath the turbulence.

Understanding elemental Vata energy provides a framework for achieving health and harmony physically, mentally, emotionally and spiritually. While mobile Vata enables change and progress, it also requires consistent nurturing and balance. Through mindfully sustaining Vata equilibrium, we maintain the flexibility, enthusiasm and alertness that allow both vibrant material living and pursuit of higher goals.

2.2 Characteristics of Pitta Dosha

The second elemental life force in Ayurveda is Pitta dosha, composed of fire and water elements. As the dosha of transformation, Pitta governs metabolism, digestion, assimilation of nutrients and body temperature regulation. Pitta provides the heat and chemistry that transforms matter into energy and sustains life processes.

The primary qualities of Pitta are hot, sharp, liquid, spreading and subtle. Additional attributes include light, oily, pungent and acidic. When functioning smoothly, Pitta promotes intelligence, understanding, courage, soft-spokenness and leadership. Out of balance, Pitta turns into fiery anger, criticism, domination or jealousy.

Pitta predominantly resides in the small intestine, stomach, liver, spleen, blood, sweat glands and eyes. Imbalances first accumulate in these areas leading to problems like indigestion, rashes, nausea, nearsightedness or anemia. During adolescence and midlife when metabolism peaks, Pitta surges in the body and mind.

Physiologically, Pitta governs digestive acids like hydrochloric acid that enable breaking down food and absorption of nutrients. Bile secretions that emulsify fats also fall under Pitta's domain. In the blood, Pitta regulates hemoglobin, white blood cells and platelet levels while governing the immune response. Pitta provides bodily heat that creates a temperature of 98.6 F optimally suited for metabolic processes and enzymatic reactions.

Mentally, Pitta rules comprehension, focus, memory and discrimination. A sharp intellect, leadership abilities, attention to detail and technical skills arise from balanced Pitta. However, too much Pitta engenders criticism, anger, competitiveness and perfectionism. Reducing inflammatory Pitta brings emotional moderation, agreeableness and cool-headed perspectives.

Those with ample Pitta typically have a medium, muscular build and put on muscle easily. They tend towards a fair or ruddy complexion, with reddish hair and freckles. Their appetite and thirst are intense, and they frequently have loose stools. They perspire heavily with a pungent odor. Pitta types dislike heat and are prone to rashes or sunburns. Mentally they have quick comprehension and very focused mental energy.

People who have a prominent Pitta dosha have a fiery passionate nature. They tend to be ambitious leaders who think clearly, debate strongly and strive for high achievement in competitive environments. Coolness, hydration and sweetness balance sharp, hot, pungent Pitta dosha.When Pitta is balanced, it confers strong digestion, sharp intellect, courage, warm emotions and leadership qualities. As the force of transformation, Pitta promotes metabolism, assimilation of nutrients and change on all levels. However, accumulated Pitta produces tendencies like fiery anger, criticism, jealousy and perfectionism.

Signs of excess Pitta in the mind and body include heartburn, ulcers and hyperacidity. The skin manifests rashes, acne and pigmentation. There is often excess body heat and hot flashes. Pitta imbalances lead to peptic ulcers and loose, burning stools. Mentally, impatience, irritability and anger issues arise. Competitiveness, control issues and jealousy emerge. People develop hyper-focus and perfectionistic tendencies.

Pitta imbalances arise from overexposure to sunlight, excessive heat, eating hot spicy foods, chronic anger and competitiveness. Cooling, hydrating foods like salads, sweet fruits and dairy soothe aggravated Pitta. Routines minimizing heat, multitasking and confrontations prevent Pitta buildup. Relaxation, sweet herbals and meditation calm excess mental fire.

Seasonally, Pitta accumulates in the blood during the hot summer months and monsoons. Overheating causes lethargy, skin irritation, irritability and indigestion in Pitta dominant people. Protecting themselves from temperature spikes through air conditioning, cold beverages and coconut water is essential. Cooling blood purifiers like coriander, fennel and aloe vera pacify Pitta in summer.

While balanced Pitta strengthens immunity, excessive Pitta cooks the blood resulting in inflammatory conditions and compromised resistance. Hot inflammatory skin disorders often signal overloaded Pitta burning the deeper blood and plasma tissues. Reducing systemic Pitta prevents inflammatory immune issues.

Imbalanced Pitta also disturbs hormones, enzymes and metabolism throughout the body systems. Cleansing and cooling the overheated liver and small intestine improves many Pitta imbalances. Blood purification also calms excess Pitta systemically.

To balance Pitta emotionally, fiery feelings of anger, hate, jealousy and hostility must be addressed through positive habits and psychology. Confidence, purpose and joy arise from harmonized Pitta. Cooling practices like moon gazing and loving-kindness soothe the angry Pitta mind.

In summary, lifestyle changes that reduce intake of Pitta provoking foods, stimulants, sunlight, competitiveness and anger restore Pitta to equilibrium. The vital fire of Pitta brings illumination when harnessed skillfully.

2.3 Characteristics of Kapha Dosha

The third elemental life force in Ayurveda is Kapha dosha, composed of earth and water. Representing structure and cohesion, Kapha provides the solidity and stability that supports the body and mind. The heavy, dense, moist qualities of Kapha balance the light, mobile, dry qualities of Vata and the hot, intense, fluid qualities of Pitta.

When balanced, Kapha promotes strength, endurance, patience, calmness and loyalty. Out of balance, Kapha leads to weight gain, attachment, greed and possessiveness. Oily, cold, heavy, dense, soft and static are key Kapha attributes. Psychologically, Kapha provides the steady continuity that allows sustained effort and tranquility.

Physically, Kapha forms the body's structural tissues like bones, muscles, tendons and fat. Within the chest, Kapha accumulates in the lungs and heart to govern respiration, cardiac function and circulation. The stomach, tongue, nasal passages and sinuses contain abundant Kapha as protective mucus membranes.

In the mind, Kapha produces the stable memories, thoughts and emotions that provide rootedness, patience and maturity. Balanced Kapha confers a reliable, consistent intellect and approach to life. When obstructed, dull Kapha causes lethargy, attachment and resistance to change.

Those with predominant Kapha tendencies often have a solid, heavier build with good musculature. They tend towards weight gain if inactive. Their skin is cool, pale, and often moist or oily. They have thick, wavy, oily hair prone to dandruff. While slow starting, Kaphas possess excellent endurance. Their personality is tranquil and steady - they dislike change. Mentally, they are methodical thinkers who learn through repetition.

The heavy, dense qualities of Kapha make it the slowest dosha to accumulate and aggravate, but also the slowest to pacify once disturbed. Lightness, dryness and stimulation counterbalance Kapha through diet, lifestyle and environment. Understanding one's innate Kapha tendencies provides a framework for achieving optimal wellbeing.When balanced, earthy Kapha provides the bodily strength, endurance and grounding that allows Vata's mobility and Pitta's intensity to operate smoothly. However, excess Kapha leads to congestion, weight gain, edema, mucus, attachment and resistance to change. Reducing heavy, cold, damp and static Kapha influences brings lightness and dynamism.

Common signs of excess Kapha include weight gain, edema, puffy eyes, fatigue, lethargy, prolonged sleepiness, sinus congestion, cough, excess mucus, cold clammy hands and feet, oily skin and hair, cystic acne, difficulty waking and getting moving, dislike of exercise unless gradual progression, emotional attachment, greed, envy, aversion to change, and getting stuck in routines.

Kapha accumulates through overeating sweet, salty and oily foods, sleeping during the day, napping after meals and a sedentary lifestyle. Cold, damp weather and environments aggravate Kapha. Light, dry, warming foods like hot cereals, ginger and pumpkin decrease Kapha's heavy qualities. Gentle yoga and meditation stimulate accumulated Kapha.

Seasonally, excess Kapha peaks in late winter and spring as the cold dampness provokes congestion, respiratory issues, weight gain and water retention. Spring detoxification helps prevent stagnation. While excellent for building youthful vitality, too much Kapha leads to congestion in the lungs, sinuses, pancreas, kidneys and joints. Eliminating excess fluids and toxins reduces this congestion.

The heavy aspects of Kapha tend to drag energy downwards, resulting in fatigue, depression, pessimism and weight gain. Lightening this through stimulation, exercise and sattvic environments uplifts the Kapha spirit. Kapha's stability can also become stubborn rigidity and resistance to change, both mentally and physically. Encouraging flexibility through new experiences evolves this tendency.

Excessive attachment in relationships leads to possessiveness, greed and envy for Kapha. Developing inclusive, detached love expands limited Kapha sentiment. The heavy aspects of Kapha also cross over into the spiritual realm as materialism, doubts and clouded consciousness. Meditation, mantra and gaining higher perspective help lighten these dense qualities.

In summary, those with Kapha constitutions thrive through dynamic routines, light foods, dryness, warmth, moderate stimulation, evolving mental patterns and detached loving presence. Flow, growth and giving balance Kapha's innate density. With mindfulness, its steady strength builds stable, compassionate living.

2.4 Determining Your Doshic Makeup

Each person is born with a unique combination of Vata, Pitta and Kapha known as their Prakruti or constitution. Prakruti determines one's inherent strengths, vulnerabilities and tendencies on all levels of life. Understanding your Prakruti offers profound insights for achieving optimal health through alignment with your inherent nature.

Ayurveda prescribes individualized recommendations for diet, routine, herbs, yoga, living environment and more based upon each person's unique proportions of the doshas. Supporting the aggravation-prone doshas while countering the excessive ones restores ideal equilibrium. Specific lifestyle adjustments to balance current doshic imbalances lead back to Prakruti's ideal state.

Prakruti is fixed at conception according to Parents' doshas, time of year, and karma or destiny. However, the interaction between unchanging Prakruti and variable internal and external influences shapes the fluctuating health and imbalance patterns throughout life. Determining Prakruti and its perpetual dance with other forces provides an Ayurvedic foundation.

There are seven primary Prakriti types depending on the dominant dosha/s:

Vata, Pitta, Kapha, Vata-Pitta, Vata-Kapha, Pitta-Kapha, Vata-Pitta-Kapha

The doshic ratios present at birth do not vary throughout life. But environment, age, lifestyle, emotions, injuries and disease trigger the doshas to fluctuate both cyclically and through longer imbalanced phases. Each doshic type has tendencies requiring counterbalancing measures to preserve equilibrium.

There are extensive signs in the physical constitution, personality traits, habitual patterns, weaknesses and health history that reveal Prakruti. An Ayurvedic practitioner thoroughly assesses these clinical indicators through intake interviews, questionnaires, evaluation of physical characteristics, and pulse analysis.

However, you can start determining your innate Prakruti through self observation of long standing patterns. Keeping a journal noting mental and emotional states, chronic issues, weather/food reactions, sleep cycles, elimination habits, endurance levels, fears, dreams and compulsions offers clues. Recording symptoms and correlating aggravations and reliefs to seasonal, dietary and lifestyle factors helps detect constitutional leanings over time.

Physical attributes provide important Prakruti clues. Those with predominant Vata are often thin, light, lean, dry or wrinkled skin, dark hair and eyes, and quick, erratic movements. Pitta types frequently have reddish complexion and hair, warm oily skin, sharp intense eyes, moderate weight and perspire easily. Kaphas tend towards thick, wavy hair, pale, cool, oily skin, large frame and movements, and heavier set build.

Doshic tendencies also manifest in digestion, elimination, and endurance patterns. Vatas have variable appetite and digestion, dry stools, and low endurance. Pittas have strong hunger and digestion, loose stools, and moderate endurance. Kaphas often skip meals, have slow digestion, tend towards constipation, and have high endurance. Mental and emotional traits also align with dosha types.

Weather and seasonal impacts provide insight into Prakruti. For example, Vatas aggravate in cold dry weather while Pittas thrive. Kaphas accumulate in cool damp seasons. Reactions to different foods, spices, environments and times of day also reflect constitutional proclivities. Discerning these innate patterns helps formulate balancing strategies.

While bio-individuality makes each Prakruti unique, the foundational dosha framework offers personalized guidance. Reviewing family history is also useful, as many constitutional attributes are inherited. With applied awareness, you can identify your distinct doshic signature. An Ayurvedic practitioner then expertly elicits subtler Prakruti insights to craft optimal wellness protocols.While identifying your predominant dosha or doshas offers insights, Prakruti determination requires looking beyond surface traits to core constitutional patterns. For example, a lifelong tendency towards anxiety likely indicates excess Vata. However, some anxiety may arise from high Pitta or Kapha temporarily displaced by stressors. Only enduring attributes reflect inborn Prakruti.

Therefore, discernment is required to distinguish between current Vikruti imbalances versus ingrained Prakruti patterns. Vikruti is the changeable condition of the doshas due to time, season, age, location, diet, lifestyle and emotions among other variables. These shifting influences disturb balance and must be managed to maintain equilibrium.

Prakruti endures as the baseline constitution, while various Vikruti patterns come and go throughout life. For example, the Prakruti may be Pitta-Kapha, but a Vikruti of disturbed Vata manifests for a period due to aging, grief or exhaustion. Once the triggers return to normal, excess Vata symptoms subside, revealing the native Pitta-Kapha Prakruti again.

Both Prakruti and Vikruti require alignment strategies. Pacifying occasional Vikruti aggravations provides symptomatic relief of acute imbalances. But following long-term recommendations for your inborn Prakruti builds deeper constitutional harmony for optimal lifelong health. Careful assessment clarifies whether indications reflect current Vikruti or enduring Prakruti.

Extensive Ayurvedic training and clinical experience allows practitioners to discern Prakruti from layers of variable Vikrutis. Certain key signals help uncover the fixed constitution, like childhood medical history that reveals innate strengths and vulnerabilities, chronic recurring issues that point to Prakruti imbalances, conditions present at birth or early childhood that reflect Prakruti, and traits consistently displayed over decades that indicate Prakruti patterns.

Vikruti dosha imbalances shift throughout seasons, ages and situations. Recognizing these tendencies helps manage transitional imbalances at each life stage. Innumerable extrinsic factors like diet, medications, trauma, temperature extremes or grief can all temporarily disturb dosha equilibrium as well.

Ayurveda's great value lies in its ability to first identify fixed Prakruti patterns, and then overlay transient Vikruti triggers and tendencies to formulate care. Healing protocols both align with innate constitution for long-term wellbeing, while normalizing current imbalances for symptomatic relief. This multi-layered assessment and treatment approach underlies Ayurveda's precision and effectiveness.

While assessing Prakruti and Vikruti can be complex, noticing consistent lifelong traits versus short-term symptoms provides initial orientation. Both require alignment, using food, herbs, routine design, yoga and other modalities to engender constitutional integrity and inner harmony. An Ayurvedic practitioner deeply investigates these subtle dynamics before making recommendations.

2.5 Achieving Doshic Balance

Understanding one's unique proportions of Vata, Pitta and Kapha doshas provides the foundation for achieving optimal balance. Our inherent doshic makeup encodes constitutional strengths, vulnerabilities and tendencies on physical, mental and emotional levels. By keeping the doshas aligned with Prakruti, we sustain positive health and inner harmony.

Each dosha thrives when supported appropriately through lifestyle factors like diet, daily rhythms, environment, relationships and more. However, inappropriate lifestyle choices disturb the doshas, leading to negative mind-body consequences over time. Ayurveda provides ancient wisdom for skillfully managing the doshas.

Some core principles help maintain equilibrium:

Like Increases Like - Choices that have similar qualities to a particular dosha will increase it. For example, cold dry foods and climate provoke light, mobile, dry Vata. We must identify qualities that pacify and balance each predominant dosha.

Opposite Decreases - Opposing qualities counterbalance accumulated doshas. Hot, oily foods reduce high Vata; cool, dry foods reduce high Pitta; dry, light foods reduce high Kapha. This forms the basis of antidotal therapy in Ayurveda.

Moderation Prevents Extremes - Staying mild and moderate in all habits prevents the radicalization of doshas. Too much sensory input, food, activity or stillness leads to excess. Judicious moderation sustains balance.

Routine Supports Flow - Following daily and seasonal routines aligns lifestyle with nature's cycles essential for harmony. Regularity counters Vata irregularity, discipline calms Pitta intensity, and dynamism stimulates Kapha inertia.

A trained Ayurvedic practitioner skillfully evaluates the interplay of your Prakruti with current Vikruti influences to determine ideal balancing measures. However, you can start bringing doshas into balance through gentle self-care aligned with Ayurvedic wisdom.

Nourishing the senses and stabilizing routine soothes unsteady Vata. Physical comfort, emotional warmth, gentle sounds, soft visual stimuli, and sweet soothing aromas ground Vata's airy lightness. Regularity around sleep, meals and activity offsets Vata's erratic nature.

Cooling and hydrating the mind-body tempers the hot intensity of Pitta. Foods, herbs and lifestyle habits that reduce heat while providing moisture, joy and relaxation settle Pitta emotions. Mint, cucumber, coconut, moonlight walks and swimming pacify excess internal and environmental heat.

Lightening heavy, slow qualities dispels stagnant Kapha. Dynamism, warmth, dryness, light textures, spicy food, exercise and stimulation counter dense inertia. Allowing structured habits to evolve prevents rigid stagnation. Newness, change and selfless service help circulate stuck Kapha energy.

While general guidelines help balance each dosha, personalized needs based on your Prakruti's unique ratios require an Ayurvedic clinician's precise recommendations. For example, a Pitta-Kapha individual needs less heat reduction than a purely Pitta type. An Ayurvedic practitioner perceives the subtle dynamics at play and custom designs care accordingly.Beyond basics like food and lifestyle, Ayurveda has countless sophisticated modalities for customized balancing of Vata, Pitta and Kapha. Under an Ayurvedic practitioner's guidance, you can experience the depths of this profound science.

Herbal medicine forms a cornerstone of doshic balancing therapy. Complex herbal formulations called Rasayanas address constitutional imbalances at tissue levels. Alterative herbs like manjistha, neem, guduch,i and amalaki remove toxins while gently rebalancing doshas.

For example, the renowned triphala formula alleviates excess Pitta and Kapha while gently promoting elimination. Churnas are powdered herb blends taken with hot water or honey that rectify many issues like high Vata constipation or Kapha congestion. Guggulu formulations reduce elevated Kapha and medhya Rasayanas like brahmi and gotu kola pacify high Vata in the mind.

Beyond herbs, mineral compounds and precious gems complement vibrational healing properties with dosha-balancing actions. Digestive salts like Hingvastak enkindle metabolic fires. Heating minerals like guggulu and loha bhasma scrape excess Kapha from tissues. Cooling moonstone and pearls calm Pitta while energizing natural rubies boost depleted Vata.

External Ayurvedic treatments offer innumerable remedies for dosha management. Abhyanga is a whole body massage with herbalized oils that deeply nourishes tissues while calming the nervous system. The oil composition is carefully crafted for the dosha imbalance and constitution. Vata-soothing sesame, Pitta-cooling coconut, Kapha-drying safflower oils are common bases.

Swedana is a steam bath, sauna or sweat inducing wrap that opens bodily channels for improved circulation while melting away accumulated doshas in the deepest tissues. Udvartana employs dry herbal powders with oil for deep exfoliation to reduce Kapha and Kapha-aggravated Vata.

Panchakarma is the most comprehensive therapy for profound constitutional balancing through dosha-specific methods of cleansing, purification and rejuvenation. Panchakarma's combination of massage, steam, herbs, heat, nutrition, relaxation and oleation therapy restores ideal doshic ratios for optimal wellbeing.

Beyond physical interventions, ancestral healing practices like mantras, rituals, gems, colors, aromas, music and astrology provide vibrational balancing of the doshas. Sound, light, design and intention influence the subtle energy systems that shape the doshas. Aromatherapy with dosha-specific essential oils harmonizes emotions, nerves and prana.

Yoga asanas, pranayama breathing techniques, bandhas, mudras and meditation offer further avenues to quiet excesses of the doshas. For example, calming forward folds, exhales and Octopus mudra reduce hyperexcitable Vata. Pitta-soothing hip openers, moon salutations and sheetali pranayama cool down intensity. Twists, backbends and kapalabhati energize stagnant Kapha. A personalized yoga program balances constitution and condition.

Lastly, maintaining sattva through lifestyle choices nurtures harmony between the physical, energetic and mental bodies where the doshas interact. Spending time in nature, listening to classical music, selfless service, gardening, cooking, laughing with friends and other activities purified of negativity balance all doshas effortlessly.

With guidance on these targeted modalities, you gain access to the most refined, nuanced, tailor-made protocols for optimizing health and wellbeing through constitutional balance. An Ayurvedic practitioner skillfully perceives the interconnected dynamics at play and prescribes precise interventions to restore wholistic harmony.

2.6 When Doshas Become Imbalanced

While your natural Prakruti proportions of Vata, Pitta and Kapha remain lifelong, temporary dosha imbalances frequently arise due to unhealthy lifestyle choices, emotional stress, trauma, seasonal changes, and other influences. Recognizing the signs of aggravated doshas empowers you to restore equilibrium through Ayurvedic self-care.

As the principle of mobility in mind and body, Vata is especially vulnerable to disturbance. Excess Vata tends to manifest as nervousness, anxiety, racing thoughts, insomnia or interrupted sleep, bloating, gas, constipation, lower back pain, sciatica, muscle spasms, fatigue, low stamina, brain fog, tremors, tingling, and absent mindedness with difficulty concentrating.

Aggravating factors like cold, dry climates, constant travel, skipping meals, exhaustion, overstimulation, grief and aging provoke high Vata. Counteracting with warmth, hydration, rest, gentle daily rhythms and Vata-soothing foods and herbs rebalances unsteady Vata.

Symptoms of excess hot, intense Pitta arising include heartburn, acid reflux, ulcers, skin rashes, inflamed acne, hives, diarrhea or burning stools, excess body heat, inflammatory conditions, sharp anger, criticism, jealousy, intense irritability and frustration, perfectionism, control issues, and competitiveness.

Pitta is aggravated by spicy foods, alcohol, smoking, excessive heat or sunlight, chronic anger and infections. Cooling off with hydration, raw juices, sweet fruits, coconut, aloe, mint and Pitta-soothing herbs like Ashwagandha and Brahmi brings fiery Pitta under control.

When heavy, dense, static Kapha accumulates excessively, it exhibits as weight gain, fluid retention, swollen joints, depression, sadness, melancholy, lethargy and excessive sleep, sinus congestion, mucus, coughs, digestive sluggishness and constipation, attachment, possessiveness, greed, and resistance to exercise and new experiences.Kapha excesses arise through overeating sweets, rich foods and dairy, napping after meals, sedentary habits, cold damp weather, and melancholic emotions. Lightening dense Kapha requires stimulation, exercise, fasting, dry heat and plenty of movement.

Imbalances result when disproportionate patterns of lifestyle, environment, emotions or seasonal changes aggravate specific doshas. For example, a stressful workplace with excessive multitasking and air conditioning provokes Vata. The hot summer sun intensifies Pitta. A cold rainy winter aggravates Kapha. Identifying excess dosha triggers allows us to counterbalance appropriately.

In addition, certain key times of life lead to predictable dosha elevations as the natural qualities in our mind-body shift. Childhood's growth spurts increase Kapha. Puberty and menses accumulate Vata through hormonal fluctuations. Adulthood's fiery passions and pursuit of goals intensifies Pitta. The dryness and increased nerves of older years vitiates Vata. Knowing essential life stage influences provides perspective when doshas become imbalanced.

Similarly, the seasons cycle through periods of aggravated Vata, Pitta and Kapha based on the qualities manifesting in nature each month. Late winter's cold and stormy wind exacerbates dry Vata. Summer's heat ignites fiery Pitta. The cool moist months of late winter and spring increase watery Kapha. Anticipating these climatic effects allows us to proactively balance doshas instead of being caught off guard.

A Comprehensive Journey into Ayurvedic Healing

When performing appropriate seasonal Panchakarma treatments to cleanse excess doshas, we sustain equilibrium through seasonal variations. For example, oleation to soothe Vata in autumn, blood purifying for Pitta in summer heat, and fasting Kapha in early spring prevent seasonal buildup turning into chronic imbalances. Undertaking maintenance aligns us with the wisdom of nature's rhythms.

Imbalanced doshas often negatively impact digestion and elimination first. When Vata slows, constipation results. Excess Pitta creates diarrhea and hyperacidity. Congested Kapha produces heavy mucus. These provide early clues to address dosha excesses through improved diet and lifestyle habits. Rekindling digestion and absorption nurtures balance systemically.

On mental and emotional levels, the excessive doshas turn traits into distortions. Anxious, fearful Vata becomes nervous exhaustion. Decisive, competitive Pitta warps into corrosive anger. Calm, centered Kapha morphs into depressive apathy. Countering these negative mind states through spiritual practices re-establishes sattva and insight.

Certain constitutional types are prone to habitual imbalances in their dominant dosha. However, when managed through wise routines, we evolve past inborn tendencies into higher balance. Loving support and conscious growth heals traumatic imprints that perpetuate distortions. Our vulnerabilities become assets on the path to self-realization.

In summary, dosha aggravation provides feedback about areas needing attention - vitiated Vata points to insufficient rest, elevated Pitta signals excessive heat, expanded Kapha reveals inadequate stimulation. Doshas speak the language of nature's elements. Harness these signals with care and heightened awareness to gracefully restore balance within primordial rhythms.

Chapter 3

An Ayurvedic Diet: Eating for Balance

3.1 Ayurvedic Dietary Guidelines

Food is life. Ayurveda offers profound insight on how to wield nature's edible abundance for optimal health, vitality and inner balance. By customizing a diet according to your mind-body type and current state of balance, Ayurvedic nutrition provides a powerful foundation for wellbeing.

Several key principles guide wise eating in Ayurveda:

Balance the Six Tastes - Each meal balances nutritional needs through sweet, sour, salty, bitter, pungent and astringent tastes. Different foods offer medicinal benefits from their elemental combinations.

Favor Fresh & Seasonal - Locally harvested, organic fruits and vegetables in season confer optimal prana or vitality. Avoid old, processed and canned foods.

Kindle Agni - Warming, pungent spices like ginger, black pepper, cumin and coriander stimulate digestion and nutrient absorption. Never drink icy beverages which shock the digestive fire.

Easy to Digest - Cooked, whole foods are best, especially grains, lentils and vegetables. Raw salads and cold foods disturb digestion unless one has an exceptionally strong agni.

Mindful Mealtimes - Eating in a calm relaxed state aids absorption and assimilation. Take a moment to offer gratitude before meals. Wait at least 2-3 hours after eating before lying down.

Until Satisfied - Follow internal hunger signals rather than external rules about portions. Stop before becoming too full. Fill half the stomach with food, a quarter with water and leave a quarter empty for optimal digestion.

Suitable Food Combining - Strategically combining foods aids digestion and absorption. For example, starch with protein is heavy and meat with dairy is difficult to digest. However, grains nicely complement vegetables and legumes.

These broad guidelines establish an Ayurvedic approach to eating. However, personal needs vary greatly based on your constitution, current state of imbalance, age, digestive capacity, activity level and stage in seasonal rhythms. A Vata type in autumn requires very different food choices than a Pitta individual feeling summer's heat. An Ayurvedic practitioner skillfully counsels each person's ideal diet.

General recommendations include nourishing the body with plenty of healthy fats like ghee, greater intake of easily digestible carbs from rice and cooked vegetables versus raw salads, and reducing ice cold foods and drinks that hamper digestion. Herbs and spices are liberally used for enhancing nutrition as well as balancing doshas.

Cooking also matters in Ayurveda. Most foods are gently cooked to increase absorption and decrease any negative effects of raw qualities. Options like soups, stews, sautéed veggies, rice pilafs and curries allow full unlocking of food's nourishment. Quick steaming or blanching helps detoxify certain vegetables before eating. Only people with excellent digestion thrive on raw foods.

Eating while emotionally balanced and sitting in a calm unrushed state improves assimilation. Certain food combinations can stress digestion so appropriate combinations should be followed. And overeating til feeling stuffed strains the entire physiology. Light and early evening meals are best.

These Ayurvedic diet insights will transform your relationship with food from haphazard to sacred. You'll gain understanding of nutritional subtleties from elemental compositions to gut microbiome balance. Proper diet and digestion fortify health from the cellular level up, protecting and prolonging wellbeing.While Ayurveda recognizes the powerful influence of food on the mind and body, it does not promote rigid dietary dogmas. Recommendations are carefully customized for your unique physiology and needs. Certain general suggestions align for most people most of the time to create a template. However, personalization is key. For example, light beans, vegetables and grains suit Vata types who tend towards variable digestion, while smaller meals with ginger tea aid sluggish digestion. Those with rapid metabolism and strong hunger are given larger portions of nourishing carbs, fats and protein. Cooling foods pacify Pitta while warmth kindles Kapha agni. The same meal may aggravate one person yet balance another.

A foundation of primordial wisdom guides appropriate application of dietary principles. Everything in moderation including moderation – too much even of healthy foods disrupts balance. When diet is wrong, medicine is of no use – nutrition provides the building blocks of health at a core level. We become what we eat – subtle impressions and qualities of food shape mind and body. Food be thy medicine – intelligently chosen foods prevent and treat disorders. Let food be thy medicine, not medicine be thy food – diet optimizes health, allowing less reliance on medicines. What type of food to eat depends on individual, place, time and culture – personalize diet aligned to constitution, climate, seasons and habits. As per capacity of digestion, food taken gets digested - overeating strains digestion, reducing nourishment gained.

These insights temper modern diet fads, conflicts and confusions. Ayurveda embraces the deeper wisdom of nature's nourishment tailored through each person's embodiment. Beyond physical nutrition, sattvic diet and conscious eating provide subtle sustenance. Negatively prepared or processed foods accumulate discordant energies. Offering gratitude before meals transforms the energies before consuming. Keeping a serene state of mind while eating allows full nutritional benefit without digestive strain from heightened emotions.

Fasting gives digestive organs deep rest while eliminating stored toxins. For non-Kaphas, light monthly fasting with only kitcheri and broths reinforces inner purification. Seasonal fasting after winter and summer enhances inner ecology. Pure nourishment sustains us while cleansing impurities. Ayurvedic nutrition manuals also prescribe appropriate foods through seasonal variations, ages of life, and women's cycles. The Ayurvedic diet crafts structural harmony and clear functioning from gross food substances all the way through refined levels of prana and consciousness.

3.2 Foods for Vata, Pitta, and Kapha

Balancing nutrition for your unique mind-body type is essential in Ayurveda. Understanding elemental qualities of foods equips us to pacify excessive doshas or kindle deficient ones as needed.

Light, dry, mobile Vata requires grounding through sweet, sour, salty foods with moist, heavy, warming qualities. Abundant good fats like ghee, protein for sustained energy, cooked vegetables and easily digested grains become Vata-soothing staples. Vatas avoid cold foods, raw salads, fruits and juices. Spices aid digestion.

Recommended Vata foods include rice, oats, cooked wheat and quinoa for grains. Warm milk, ghee, cream, butter, and soft cheese are suitable dairy. Ripe bananas, avocados, mangoes, and peaches are recommended fruits. Cooked beets, carrots, asparagus, okra are good vegetables. Eggs, turkey, chicken, fish, nuts provide protein. Mung beans, lentils, and urad dal are ideal legumes. Good oils for Vata are ghee, sesame, almond, and olive. Cinnamon, cumin, ginger, garlic, basil are beneficial herbs.

Sweet juicy fruits and cooked veggies with warming spices provide needed gentleness for Vata. Avoiding raw, cold, dry foods prevents vitiating mobile Vata. Meals should be satiating, nourishing, and comfortable. Routines stay regular, and Vatas skip meals only with care as an empty stomach aggravates Vata. Bedtime is early.

Pitta's fiery intensity benefits from cool, heavy, moist foods. Bitter and astringent tastes balance Pitta. Raw vegetables, salads, fruits, and greens extinguish heat. Cooling coconut, cucumber, mint soothe fiery Pitta. Avoid sour, acidic or fermented foods. Generous water prevents dehydration.

Ideal Pitta foods include white Basmati rice, barley, oats, wheat for grains. Milk, butter, ghee, ice cream are good dairy. Sweet melons, mangoes, peaches, plums, figs are recommended fruits. Leafy greens, broccoli, celery, okra, asparagus are suitable vegetables. Chicken, eggs, fish, nuts, tofu provide protein. Mung beans, chickpeas are beneficial legumes. Coconut, sunflower, olive, ghee are good oils. Coriander, fennel, mint, cardamom are recommended herbs.

Kapha's heavy, slow qualities lighten through dry, warming, pungent foods with bitter, astringent and pungent tastes. Light grains, vegetables and legumes aid mobility. Lean proteins energize. Stimulating spices ignite metabolic fire. Foods to balance dense Kapha include barley, buckwheat, millet, quinoa, amaranth for grains. Turkey, chicken, eggs, beans, tofu, cod, tuna provide protein. Mustard, sunflower, sesame, and safflower are suitable oils. The same meal could imbalance Vata but satisfy Kapha and Pitta. Personalizing foods aligned with Prakruti and current state prevents disorder.While general guidelines help choose foods that balance common dosha traits, individual variability requires personalized fine tuning. An Ayurvedic clinician skillfully assesses not just your Prakruti but also Agni digestive strength, age, activity level, seasonal changes, and current Vikruti imbalances to provide customized dietary guidance.

For example, a fiery Pitta with low Agni requires smaller, easier to digest meals despite intensity of appetite. Cool, heavy foods are prescribed for hyperactive Pitta only when digestion is very robust. Mild herbs and spices kindle weaker Agni while small portions prevent overwhelming it. Those who tend towards loose stools or hyperacidity receive carminative herbs in meals along with Pitta soothing foods.

Vata constitution individuals with anxiety, fatigue or weak Agni need an abundance of building foods like milk, ghee and boundary-setting routines around meals. More mobile, restless Vata types pursue dynamic activities requiring protein, complex carbs and nutrients for active tissues. Light vegetarian foods fuel moderate activity in dry climates while cold climates demand hot soups and heavier fare.

Stagnant, overweight Kapha types receive light, dry, pungent food prescriptions. But drier climates or high exertion occupations necessitate additional good oils to hydrate the mobile Vata that accumulates through activity. Cool, calm Kaphas in damp environments need extra stimulation from exercise, spices and bitter herbs. Those prone to hypoglycemia require frequent small meals.

While purified foods nourish and gently detoxify, processed foods vitiate the doshas. However, Vatas who use stimulants like coffee find slow weaning off aids long-term balance. Removing all dietary restrictions makes excess cravings subside. Gentle retraining returns to sattvic eating without self-judgement.

Bhutas are the five elements manifesting in food. Less processed items retain beneficial prana not just nutritional content. However, modern environmental toxins require selective buying even for whole foods. Organic, local, pesticide-free, chemical-free and non-GMO foods provide the highest quality nutrient sources.

Freshness matters as much as ingredients. Enzymatic integrity of whole foods rapidly depletes with wilting, freezing, aging or microwaving. Buying frequent small amounts of produce preserves prana through quick use. Frozen fruits and vegetables retain nutrition better than canned which becomes tamasic through processing. Avoid leftovers kept beyond a day.

Balancing taste and elemental qualities provides eight pillars of dietary harmony. Food combining aids digestion. Proper cooking and spice alchemy enhances assimilation of nutrients. Meal ambiance with calm presence influences how nourishment is received. Synchronizing with circadian rhythms grants maximum benefits from ingested foods.

The Ayurvedic nutrition approach allows intuitive eating aligned with inner Agni signals. Our physiology guides us when seeking balance through natural whole foods. With awareness, we learn to properly feed our unique embodiment for optimal wellbeing. Diet becomes part of holistic living, not a restrictive dogma.

3.3 Seasonal Eating and Menu Planning

Beyond choosing foods that balance your constitution, Ayurveda recommends aligning diet with nature's seasonal rhythms and solar cycles. As light, temperature, moisture and qualities shift from month to month, certain foods, spices and routines promote harmony at different times of year.

Spring's cool, muddy Kapha period requires lighter fare like grains and legumes cooked with warming spices, bitter herbs and pungent foods. Occasional fasting cleanses excess winter Kapha buildup. Favor foods with fiery, pungent and bitter tastes to kindle digestive Agni and dry out internal dampness before seasonal allergies strike.

Summer's heat brings Pitta's sharp, oily, spreading qualities to the fore calling for cooling foods like fruits, dairy, cucumbers and melons. Avoid sour, fermented, greasy, spicy foods that overheat the liver and blood. Generous water intake prevents dehydration. The hot sun depletes minerals and electrolytes so adequately replenishing them maintains energy through sweaty summer.

Dry, cold, erratic Vata dominates fall and early winter. Grounding, moist, oily, heavy warm foods balance Vata like cooked grains and veggies, soups, stews and oil rich foods. Additional protein sustains energy as the cold saps. Vata-pacifying breakfasts fortify for a long day. Always minimize raw, cold foods to prevent Vata aggravation.

Late winter returns to dense, heavy, wet Kapha patterns. Light, dry, warming foods get stagnant energy and lymphatics flowing. Resume vigorous exercise routines and oil massages before bed to counter lethargy and heaviness. Occasional fasting purifies excess mucus. Focus on easily digestible grains and vegetables to kindle Agni without taxing weakened digestion.

Rasayanas are rejuvenative herbs taken in seasonal rhythms to fortify against building excesses. Ashwagandha, guduchi, amalaki, haritaki, shilajit and other adaptogens boost resistance to climatic influences that disturb dosha balance. For example, amalaki pacifies excess Pitta in summer, guduchi reduces winter Kapha, and ashwaganhda calms fall Vata.

The Ayurvedic clock links dosha cycles to solar rhythms. Kapha dominates the moonlit hours till 6 am. Digestive Pitta rules from 10 am - 2 pm when the sun is strongest. Airy Vata prevails through the variable windy evenings. Dining and sleeping in tune with these phases prevents disrupting natural flows.

Local seasonal produce aligns us with the soil and environment. Fruits and vegetables grown nearby contain balancing qualities for current atmospherics. Cold climates should stick to seasonal produce and avoid importing fruits with cold energy like bananas and oranges. In warmer areas, abundant cooling coconut, cucumbers and melons restore balance naturally.

Planning weekly seasonal menus ensures incorporating suitable fruits, vegetables, herbs, and spices. For example, summer menus focus on juicy cooling fruits, ährend hydrating vegetables predominate in dry heat. Each season's distinct qualities help prevent weather-related imbalances. Pre-designed recipes streamline shopping and preparation.

Eating with awareness and gratitude sanctifies meals. Offering thanks connects us to the deeper nourishment food provides our mind-body-spirit. Shared meals strengthen family and community bonds. Preparing food while in a positive state of mind transfers those sattvic qualities into the meal. Even simple meals thus elevate into sacred rituals of self-care.Attuning to the distinctive energies and offerings of each season connects us with nature's cycles for optimal wellbeing year-round. When we harmonize activities, diet and self-care practices with seasonal qualities, balance and vitality naturally follow.

In Vasant Ritu, spring, we mirror nature's impulse of revival after winter's stagnation. Dynamic regimens, light grains, bitter herbs, and fasting reboot sluggish digestion and lymphatics congested by cold weather. Spring cleanses and renews the spirit with new endeavors after winter's inward focus.

Grishma Ritu, summer's heat, necessitates cooling, hydrating influences to counter internal and external Pitta aggravation. Abundant fresh juices, fruits, mint, cilantro and coconut soothe the fiery blood and liver. Light clothing, minimal sun exposure, swimming, and cool showers prevent overheating. Staying calm and relaxed offsets summer's intensity.

Sharad Ritu, fall's transition, requires grounding light Vata before it scatters energy. Heavy, oily, warm, nourishing foods stabilize Vata as the cold and dry return. Gentle winding down of activity ushers in introspection. Focusing projects completed before winter sets in. The fall harvest shares nature's bounty to strengthen immunity before winter.

In Shishir Ritu or early winter, we insulate from cold, wind and rain that provoke Vata imbalances. Vigorous oil massage before bedtime prevents vitiating dryness. Warm soups, stews and teas nurture the inner fire. Early nights allow extra rest to offset longer darkness. Time spent indoors and in reflection rejuvenates the mind and spirit.

The seasonal produce available in each region provides natural balance. Local plants hold innate adaptogenic intelligence for the surrounding environment. Eating indigenous grains like barley in cold climates and cooling coconuts in the tropics creates harmony. Preserving summer's harvest replenishes minerals depleted by sweat and heat.

Cooking styles can balance seasons as well. Steaming and soups warm from inside during winter. Salads and juicing generate internal coolness in summer heat. Slow cooked stews and oil rich fare provide needed heaviness in fall and spring. Ayurvedic cooking alchemizes food energetics.

A Comprehensive Journey into Ayurvedic Healing

Ritucharya therapy recommends ideal routines for preventative seasonal care. Tailoring self-care, fitness, bedtimes, work habits and relationships to the seasons flows with nature's rhythms. Yearly cleanses reset accumulated dosha excesses established through cold, heat, dryness or moisture at the junctions of seasons.

Beyond inner balance with seasonal wisdom, we gain deeper connection to the cycles continually renewing life on our planet. Flowing with astonishing transformations occurring each year restores awe at nature's majesty. Treading lightly upon the earth with reverence comes naturally when recalling our small place amidst this vast intelligent cosmos.

3.4 Herbs and Spices for Healing

Ayurveda employs a vast Materia Medica of botanical medicines tailored to each person's constitution and imbalances. Skilled use of herbs, spices and plant formulations restores balance, nourishes tissues, removes toxins and promotes longevity.

The tastes or Rasa profiles of herbs indicate their energetic actions on the physiology. Sweet, bitter and astringent decreasing Kapha. Pungent, sour and salty pacify Vata. Bitter, astringent and sweet balance Pitta. Knowledge of Rasa profiles, along with the qualities and effects of each herb, guides proper formulation.

Some common Ayurvedic herbs and spices used for healing include turmeric, cinnamon, ginger, guduchi, pepper, coriander, cumin, fennel, dill, fenugreek, cardamom, clove, amla, neem, gotu kola, brahmi, ashwagandha. Each provides unique benefits from anti-inflammatory and antioxidant effects to stimulating digestion, detoxification, rejuvenation, calming the mind and much more. Spices like ginger, cumin and turmeric kindle digestive fire. Cooling herbs such as brahmi, aloe and gotu kola pacify excess Pitta. Sweet and bitter herbs calm Vata and Kapha.

Beyond taste, Ayurveda classifies herbs according to their targeted action: Prabhava (special potency), Rasayana (rejuvenation), and Virechana (purgation). The application depends on the individual's needs. Rasayanas provide generalized rejuvenation while purgatives stimulate elimination of excess doshas.

Ayurvedic pharmacy also prepares herbs through various alchemical processes that enhance potency, like fermentation, roasting, drying, grinding, and more. Bhasmas are herbo-mineral preparations involving elaborate stepwise reactions that concentrate the subtle energy. With the extensive Ayurvedic herbal knowledge, plants offer healing gifts tailored to each person and condition, gently restoring balance without side effects.Beyond individual herbs, Ayurvedic pharmacy meticulously crafts formulas containing synergistic combinations for targeted results. The compositions are carefully balanced by an expert Vaidya to ensure maximum therapeutic potency.

For example, the renowned triphala formula mixes three fruits - haritaki, bibhitaki and amalaki - to gently cleanse the colon, strengthen digestion and eliminate ama without side effects. Churnas are powdered herb mixes like trikatu or talisadi taken with hot water to balance doshas. Avalehas are medicinal jams like chyawanprash eaten as rasayana tonics. Bhasmas deliver minerals and gem essences for subtle rejuvenation.

The vehicle or anupana carrying the herbs also matters. Most often, formulas are taken with warm water to aid absorption. But dairy, juices, teas, honey and other liquids produce specific effects that complement the herbs. Anupanas escort active compounds to target tissues swiftly and optimally.

A Comprehensive Journey into Ayurvedic Healing

With guidance, daily Ayurvedic herbal supplements support gentle inner cleansing, balanced nutrition and sustained energy. For example, Ashwagandha and Brahmi formulas reduce daily Vata and Pitta imbalances causing anxiety and compromised focus. Cooling Guduchi and Neem removes Pitta and Kapha excesses, heating the blood. Triphala maintains regular bowels and detox.

For periodic deep detoxification, Ayurveda offers more intensive herbal purgation and cleansing. Under supervision, short courses of strong herbs like Senna stimulate cleansing of accumulated ama and toxins from the colon and digestive tract. The treatment concludes with restorative tonics to rebuild tissues. Panchakarma intensifies this purging through oleation and elimination therapies.

Certain rasayanas are taken in cycles for prevention and profound nourishment. Chyawanprash eaten for 48 days rejuvenates immunity and mental functions through concentrated amla and over 40 herbs. Ashwagandha strengthens muscles, bones and reproductive tissues when taken in monthly or seasonal cycles. Brahmi enhances neuro-cognitive growth in children.

Daily consumption of Ayurvedic plant medicines progressively orchestrates transformative healing from root cause levels. Subtly selected herbs detoxify and nourish the source tissues, upgrade the metabolic pathways, kindle digestion and elimination, balance emotional biochemistry, and open natural flow in energy channels. The benefits magnify over time.

Within this Materia Medica resides the remarkable intelligence of nature, offering us her grace in plant form to rejuvenate body, mind and soul. Brush aside assumptions that herbs provide mild supplementary benefits. Their power elicits no less than profound healing on every level when applied with Ayurvedic wisdom.

A trained Ayurvedic Vaidya deftly diagnosis the core issues before selecting from over 10,000 plant possibilities the ideal single herbs or formulations to holistically restore balance. Then exact preparation methods alchemically concentrate therapeutic potencies while diminishing undesirable effects. Detailed guidance brings the internal ecosystem into harmony step-by-step.

The beauty of Ayurvedic herbalism blossoms when guided by an expert. Their vision perceives your unique path to wellbeing through ancient empirical knowledge refined over millennia. With humility, we can embrace nature's wisdom for holistic healing of body, mind and spirit. Daily discipline allows the subtle power of herbs to purify, awaken and transform you from within.

3.5 Fasting and Detoxification

Fasting and detoxification are powerful tools in the Ayurvedic toolkit for cleansing the body, mind, and spirit. Used wisely and appropriately, these practices can eliminate accumulated toxins, strengthen digestion, reset unhealthy habits, and provide deep rejuvenation.

In Sanskrit, fasting is referred to as upavasa. It generally means abstaining from or limiting food for a period of time while consuming ample fluids. Fasting gives the digestive system a profound period of rest, which in turn enhances agni (digestive fire), supports the liver and kidneys, and purifies the blood and lymph. Even the routine practice of eating lightly in the mornings and evenings serves as a mild fast, helping to regulate appetite and digestion. Periodic, more restrictive fasts provide deeper cleansing benefits.

Fasting is not advised for everyone, and the duration and intensity must be tailored to the individual. Those who are underweight, lack strength, or have serious health issues should undertake fasts only with expert guidance. For others in good health, occasional one-day fasts are usually quite safe and beneficial. Kitchari fasts involving easy-to-digest rice and bean preparations are ideal first steps for those new to fasting. Short-term fasts of 3-5 days demand more planning and care. Panchakarma purification programs at Ayurvedic retreats often incorporate 7-10 day fasting periods under close supervision of practitioners.

In preparation for a longer fast, it is wise to reduce food intake, exercise, and stimulants gradually in the preceding days. During the fast, rest as much as possible and avoid strenuous activity. Drink plenty of warm water with lemon, herbal teas, broths, juices, coconut water, or buttermilk kulambu according to your constitution. Some fasting protocols permit limited fruits and vegetables. Break the fast gradually by advancing from lighter to heavier foods over 2-3 days. Fasting concludes with a rejuvenating period of rest and integration.

The most cleansing fasts limit all foods and rely solely on water. These water-only fasts deeply rest the entire digestive tract and should be pursued cautiously. Kitchari and fruit fasts are gentler alternatives, while still providing substantial detox benefits. A kitchari fast includes eating simple mung dal kitchari made with basmati rice and yellow split mung beans cooked in ghee and spices. This nourishing, tridoshic meal gives the digestion a vacation without depleting the body.

In addition to fasting from food, consider dialing down sensory input, media consumption, talking, and sexual activity to direct energy inward. Spend fasting periods in reflection, meditation, prayer, journaling, or quiet walks in nature. Ayurveda advises minimizing negative emotions and cultivating positive ones to enhance the purification process.

Detoxification therapies known as shodhana cleanse the body at deeper levels. Panchakarma provides the most thorough detox through emesis, purgation, enemas, nasal irrigation, and blood purification procedures.

For home detox, try simpler cleansing techniques like nasya oil nasal drops, saltwater gargles, tongue scraping, oil pulling, and castor oil purgation when needed for constipation. Dry brushing and abhyanga oil massage also help mobilize toxins before bathing.

Reduce exposure to environmental toxins in your living and work spaces to ease the body's detox load. Clean up your diet by eliminating processed foods, sugars, simple carbs, unhealthy fats, alcohol, caffeine and chemical additives. Stay well-hydrated and favor lighter, easy-to-digest seasonal foods recommended for your dosha during cleanses. Herbs like guggulu, triphala, guduchi, chitrak, amalaki and turmeric support internal detoxification.

Fasting and detoxification offer renewing breaks from the habitual patterns of daily life. As you eliminate toxins and congestion, clarity naturally arises. Take this opportunity to pause, turn within, and reconnect with your true nature. Each cleanse can strengthen awareness, willpower, and inner peace. With patience and self-care, you will arise feeling purified, spacious, revitalized, and ready to embrace positive changes after fulfilling the needs of your body, mind and spirit through fasting.Food sensitivities and allergies have become increasingly common in modern times. Ayurveda offers helpful guidance for identifying problem foods and healing your digestive fire to properly metabolize foods. Certain foods provoke allergic reactions or intolerances in those with compromised digestion and weakened intestinal barriers. Symptoms range from rashes, headaches, bloating, and fatigue to severe life-threatening anaphylaxis.

While Western medicine focuses on allergy testing and avoidance, Ayurveda takes a broader, more holistic approach. Proper digestive strength (agni) and intestinal integrity form the foundation. Imbalanced agni leads to the formation of toxins (ama) that clog microchannels (srotas) and trigger inflammatory reactions. Pacifying aggravating doshas, strengthening agni, and cleansing ama are primary goals.

An elimination diet can help detect trigger foods. Track symptoms diligently while removing suspect foods for 2-4 weeks. Dairy, wheat, eggs, soy, nuts, seafood, and nightshades are common culprits. Slowly reintroduce foods one at a time while observing reactions. For diagnosed allergies, strictly avoid the provoking allergen.

Certain common food intolerances linked to genetic traits may persist lifelong. Lactose intolerance is caused by insufficient lactase enzymes needed to digest dairy. Gluten intolerance stems from an immune reaction to gliadin proteins in grains like wheat. Fructose malabsorption arises from insufficient fructose transporters in the gut. Following an individualized diet free from personal intolerances is essential.

Ayurveda classifies food into categories based on energetic qualities. Determine which food groups aggravate your unique constitution and increase inflammation. As a Pitta type, spicy, oily, or acidic foods may overheat your sensitive digestive tract. For Kaphas, heavy, fatty, or dairy-based foods could congest your system. For Vatas, gas-producing foods like beans, broccoli or carbonated drinks might create discomfort. Listen to the wisdom of your body and adjust your diet accordingly.

To rebuild intestinal integrity, emphasize easy-to-digest seasonal foods appropriate for your dosha. Favor freshly cooked, organic and local foods over canned, processed, or genetically modified options. Soak beans, grains and nuts to increase digestibility. Spice meals with ginger, cumin, coriander, fennel, and turmeric to stoke agni. Stay hydrated and sip warm water with meals. Minimize cold, frozen, greasy and heavy foods that impair digestion.

Supplementing with probiotics and digestive enzymes can replenish gut flora and bolster digestive capacity. Probiotic foods like yogurt, kefir, sauerkraut, kimchi and kombucha foster healthy intestinal bacteria. Digestive herbs such as shatavari, licorice, peppermint, cardamom and cinnamon help heal and coat the gut lining. Marma point massage and yoga poses that twist and compress the abdomen can stimulate agni and circulation.

Panchakarma cleansing under Ayurvedic guidance removes toxins and restores balance at deeper levels. Elimination diets, colon hydrotherapy, and detoxifying herbals like triphala rejuvenate the gastro-intestinal tract. Stress management is equally important since stress inhibits digestion. Activities like yoga, meditation, walks in nature and self-massage cultivate relaxation. Get plenty of rest between meals for optimal assimilation. Allowing at least 3 hours before sleep aids nighttime detoxification.

For severe food intolerances and allergies, seek advice from an experienced Ayurvedic practitioner or integrative physician. Though dietary changes and natural remedies can often significantly improve intolerances over time, medical intervention may be warranted in some cases. Together you can develop a personalized plan to heal your digestive fire, restore gut integrity, and safely expand your diet as gut health improves. With patience and diligent self-care, you can minimize reactions and recover your ability to properly digest and receive nourishment from a wide variety of wholesome foods.

3.6 Addressing Food Intolerances and Allergies

Ayurveda recommends aligning your diet and lifestyle rhythms with the perpetual cycles of nature to maintain optimal health and vitality year-round. Each season has its unique qualities and influences which are mirrored in the shifting produce availability. Eating fresh, local foods that grow naturally in each season brings you into harmony with your environment.

Spring is governed by the earth and water elements as the warming sun's rays melt winter's snows and stimulate new growth. The cooling, heavy, dense qualities help pacify accumulating pitta and kapha. Light, dry foods that decrease kapha like barley, chickpeas, honey and berries are best. Favor bitter, astringent and pungent tastes while reducing heavy, oily foods. Lighten up and stimulate digestion after winter's sedentary period.

As the hot fiery sun reaches full power, summer takes dominance expressing fire and air elements. Pitta season has a heating, penetrating influence. The diet should consist of cooling, hydrating foods like cucumbers, squash, coconut, watermelon, mint and greens to calm aggravated pitta. Reduce consumption of salty, sour and pungent fire-stoking foods. Keep the body light and comfortable by favoring easily digestible grains like rice and oats.

Autumn approaches with its earth and air energies as wind, cold and dryness increase once again. Vata prevails as the air element urges movement and circulation in the body and mind. Grounding foods like nuts, whole grains and squash stabilize erratic vata. Warming spices like ginger, black pepper and mustard stimulate digestion. Moist, sweet, sour warming foods balance cold, dry, light qualities. Soups, stews, oils, dairy and heavier grains are beneficial.

The water and earth elements crystallize in winter's cold, heavy, cloudy essence. Kapha accumulates, signaling a need for stimulating and lightening foods. Pungent, bitter, astringent foods like honey, barley, rye, basil, sprouts, chickpeas and cranberries counter kapha's density. Increase hot spices like ginger, black pepper, cayenne and mustard. Avoid cold, heavy, greasy, sweet and sour foods that can stagnate kapha. Energizing foods keep digestive fires stoked in the inactive cold months.

In addition to adjusting food qualities, observe how much you eat. Consume the largest meal midday when digestion is strongest. Take breakfast lightly to kindle metabolism after the overnight fast. Make the evening meal the lightest to avoid overtaxing digestion before bed.

Serving smaller portions prevents overeating. Leave one-fourth of the stomach empty to allow space for proper digestion. Wait until the previous meal fully digests before snacking or eating again. Honoring your natural hunger and fullness signals creates balance.

Cooking methods also vary by season. Steam or boil vegetables to retain nutrients. In winter, sautéing and baking turn up digestive heat. Marinate meats in summer to tenderize and aid digestion. Soups, stews and curries warm the body in cold seasons. Stir-frying, juicing and raw salads keep the body cool in hot weather. Ice cream, lassi and smoothies combat summer's fiery pitta state.

Rhythmic seasonal routines reorient your physiology in tune with the cadence of nature. Waking and sleeping with the sun's cycle harmonizes hormones and circadian biology. Seasonal yoga, meditation, oil massage and cleansing further prevent accumulating seasonal imbalances. Once you align dietary choices with practical seasonal wisdom, the body effortlessly maintains homeostasis despite nature's cyclical fluctuations.

While adhering to general seasonal guidelines, also tailor your eating habits to your personal constitution. Pitta types need extra cooling foods in summer when pitta aggravates most readily. Kapha predominants require more light, dry, warming foods in winter and spring when kapha accumulates. Vatas need grounding, moistening foods in windy, cold, dry autumn and late winter. An Ayurvedic practitioner can individualize seasonal diet and lifestyle guidance in accordance with your unique design.Menu planning helps translate Ayurvedic wisdom into practical daily meals aligned with seasonal and constitutional needs. Each meal can balance your dominant dosha and current state of health. Breakfast may emphasize vata-pacifying foods for those busy mornings. Lunch cools fiery pitta when the sun is strongest. Kapha-reducing, light evening meals aid sleep. While planning weekly menus, include all six Ayurvedic tastes - sweet, sour, salty, bitter, pungent and astringent - across meals for nutritional diversity.

Preparing food with love and awareness brings vastly more benefit than eating from packages. Cooked foods tend to be healthier and easier to digest than raw foods. Boiling, steaming, sautéing and baking are optimal cooking methods. Each meal centers around a hearty grain like rice, millet or quinoa along with well-cooked lentils or beans for balanced protein. Round out meals with fresh or cooked vegetables, micro-greens and salads. Add small portions of organic dairy, nuts, seeds, eggs or meats as desired for added nourishment.

For beverages, sip hot water with lemon to stimulate digestion and hydration. Fresh ginger tea aids digestion and circulation. Wholesome lassis blend yogurt with cardamom, cumin, mint or fruits. Warm milk with turmeric and honey calms nerves and eases sleep. Cooling coconut water, aloe vera juice and cucumber mint water balance summer's heat. Always favor natural, homemade drinks over artificial sodas or juices.

Desserts are medicinal opportunities to correct imbalances. Milk puddings strengthen ojas and nourish the nervous system. Cardamom and coconut ladoo candies reduce vata and kapha. Berries and pomegranates cool excess pitta. Churna cookies made with warming spices kindle agni. Avoid cold, heavy, sweet treats that impair digestion.

Wake before sunrise if possible, and eat breakfast by 7-8am. Lunch from 12-1pm fuels peak digestive power. Have a light dinner before sunset around 6-7pm. Allow 3-6 hours between meals without snacking to completely digest. Avoid overeating or rushing meals. Eat in a calm, pleasant atmosphere with soft background music. Savor each bite, chewing thoroughly to initiate digestion. A peaceful state of mind while eating improves assimilation. Say grace before meals in gratitude for nature's bounty.

Having a planned menu prepared in advance makes healthy eating effortless. Shop once weekly and prep ingredients ahead of time. Stock your pantry with staple grains, legumes, oils, dairy, spices, condiments and fresh produce. Wash and chop vegetables and herbs. Make soups, stews, curries and grains in large batches for leftovers. Portion cooked items into daily servings for fast, balanced meals throughout the week. Healthy eating becomes seamless when the components are organized and on hand. With mindful meal preparation, you ritualize caring for your unique body, mind and spirit.

Chapter 4

Ayurvedic Routines: Daily and Seasonal

4.1 Establishing a Healthy Daily Routine

The cornerstone of Ayurvedic living is aligning with natural circadian rhythms through a balanced daily routine. Dinacharya sets the day on course by honoring the body's innate biological clocks for eating, sleeping, working, resting and self-care. These optimized timetables regulate essential physiological functions, neuro-hormonal secretions and metabolic processes that underpin health, tissue integrity and longevity.

Waking before dawn is ideal to catch the vata time of mobility and fresh energy. Morning routines capitalize upon natural cycles by clearing wastes, hydrating, and igniting digestion and elimination prior to breakfast. Take a few quiet moments upon rising for prayer, meditation or contemplation to set a peaceful, intentional tone for the day.

Cleaning the senses brightens the mind. Scrape the tongue to detoxify ama from the digestive tract and freshen the palate. Swish sesame or coconut oil vigorously in the mouth for oral cleansing and strengthening gums. Massage warming sesame oil into the scalp to nourish hair follicles and sense organs. Lubricate the nasal passages with a few drops of brahmi or calamus oil.

Perform full ablutions to refresh the body, hydrate the colon and stimulate peristalsis. Drinking warm water with lemon jumpstarts the organs. Eliminate wastes to reduce bodily impurities and clear the channels for vitality. Cleanse the eyes, ears and orifices with cool water to awaken the senses. Bathe or shower using cleansing Ayurvedic herbs like chickpea flour, neem, turmeric and essential oils.

Oil massage with traditional Ayurvedic techniques (abhyanga) enhances circulation, loosens toxins, conditions joints, fortifies muscles, nourishes skin and relaxes the nervous system. Apply herbalized oils like brahmi, bhringraj or ashvagandha and massage gently into joints, marma points and extremities using circular, back-and-forth motions.

Yoga asanas and pranayama breathing exercises optimize energy, flexibility, lung capacity and mental clarity. Choose postures and breathing techniques aligned with your constitution. Move gently and modify asanas as needed. Finish with meditation or quiet reflection. Lightly stimulating vata-reducing essential oils purify the air.

Proper elimination regularizes the bowels and removes wastes. Drink hot ginger tea to aid digestion. Ingest 1-2 teaspoons of triphala churna to gently clear the colon. Alternating hot and cold hip baths stimulate apana vayu elimination. Massaging the lower abdomen with castor oil can relieve constipation when necessary.

Tongue scraping, oil pulling and gargling help cleanse the digestive tract after elimination. Rinsing the eyes, nose and mouth refreshes the head. Follow with a light, easy-to-digest breakfast favoring warm, unctuous foods. Herbal teas support digestion and elimination through the day.

Ayurvedic routines attune your intrinsic rhythms with natural cycles of change. Waking with the sun, dutiful self-care, yoga, meditation, regular elimination, light morning meals and appropriate work and rest consistently balance tridosha throughout the day.The midday sun energizes peak digestive power, demanding the largest meal when agni is strongest. Warm, nourishing, easily-digestible lunches ground erratic vata and build strength. During lighter sunset suppers, favor lighter grains, soups and cooked vegetables to avoid overtaxing nighttime digestion. Herbal digestifs like cumin, fennel, ginger, cardamom and cinnamon improve agni's efficiency.

At dusk, vata rises once again, making evenings the optimal time for self-care rituals before bed. Gentle yoga elongates tight muscles and calms the mind. Twenty minutes of meditation transports awareness from hectic daily affairs into quiet inner awareness. Channeling vitality inwards through spiritual practices prevents vata agitation at day's end.

Abhyanga coaxes vata downward through oil massage. Apply warm herbalized oil over the entire body to deeply penetrate and nourish tissues. Soothing sesame, almond, coconut or castor oils pacify vata and promote sound sleep. Lightly massaging the soles, scalp and ears grounds high vata's airy tendencies.

A warm bath, swim or time in a sauna allows oil to penetrate skin before washing away excess. Cooling moonlit walks calm fiery pitta and let go of mental tension. Listening to classical music, playing a harmonium or soft vocal chanting creates pleasantness before sleep. Let the day's exertions dissolve as you turn within.

Retire before 10pm to align with natural cycles. Darkness and silence signal rest for the senses and closure of the day. Prepare the bedroom to sanctify sleep and set the stage for rejuvenation. Remove electronic devices and distracting lights. Diffusing calming lavender, vetiver or cedarwood scent purifies the space.

Lie on the left side in darkness to pacify vata and pitta. Setting out sleep clothes and preparing the next day's outfit reduces evening vata. Going to bed with a clear plan for the morning instills a sense of order. Reading spiritual literature nurtures consciousness and dissolves anxiety. Allow worries to drift away as you surrender to sleep.

Waking and retiring with Brahma muhurta aligns biorhythms to solar and lunar cycles. Consistent early sleeping and rising times strengthen circadian regulation. Late nights disrupt serotonin, melatonin and sleep hormones that orchestrate rest. Early to bed and early to rise truly makes one healthy, wealthy and wise.

Daily routines attuned with nature's rhythms wield tremendous power to profoundly impact health and happiness. Following Ayurvedic wisdom to care for your unique mind and body each morning and evening serves as preventative medicine and sets health on the proper footing day by day, year after year.

4.2 Managing Seasonal Changes with Ritucharya

The transitions between seasons offer opportunities to realign your routine and environment as external conditions shift. Ayurveda's wisdom of ritucharya provides guidance to maintain balance through seasonal variations in weather, diet, lifestyle behaviors and inner awareness.

Spring's cool, damp, muddy qualities help clear accumulated heat, fat and toxins built up over winter. Light fasting or mono-diets of cleansing grains like barley or rice gives the digestive fire a break after heavy winter foods. Favor bitter, astringent and pungent tastes to dry excess moisture. Increase exercise and yoga to invigorate circulation and metabolism after winter's sedentary months. Stimulating essential oils like peppermint, eucalyptus and camphor open the channels and dispel lethargy.

Late spring presents hotter, drier conditions as summer nears, increasing pitta. Cooling foods like cucumbers, bitter greens, coconut and aloe vera prevent pitta irritation. Gentler exercise lowers heat production. Reduce spice and oil consumption. Swim in cool lakes to balance rising temperatures. Wear cooling light, cotton clothes in soothing pastels. Prioritize relaxation and quietude.

Summer's heat is directed inward through fasting, meditation and introspection. The outer solar fire stokes the inner digestive fire. Light, easy to digest grains, vegetables and cooling fruits temper pitta flames. Stay hydrated with coconut water, herbal teas, aloe drinks. Avoid heavy meals, fermented foods, oils and animal proteins that overheat the gut. Rosewater, sandalwood, mint and jasmine perfumes calm fiery emotions. Generosity and spirituality blossom in summer's pitta energy.

As autumn winds whip up vata's mobile air, grounding routines stabilize erratic energy. Warming soups, stews and tonifying foods build strength and immunity through seasonal change. Gentle daily oil massage protects the skin and joints from dryness. Keep warm and protected from drafts. Counter anxiety and restlessness with meditation, nature walks and soothing music. Begin transitioning toward the warmer foods, like nuts and grains, which pacify vata in winter.Ritucharya is an essential principle of Ayurveda that involves adapting our routines, diet, and lifestyle according to the qualities and energies of the current season. Aligning ourselves with nature's rhythms allows us to maintain balance through the changing seasons and avoid seasonal health imbalances.

Spring is dominated by the Kapha dosha in nature, a time of renewal, growth and flourishing. As the cool winter melts away, the environment becomes characterized by qualities of heaviness, softness, moisture and fertility. Our bodies also feel heavier and more Kapha in spring. To reduce Kapha in spring, Ayurveda recommends eating lighter, drier, warming foods like barley, rye and bitter greens. Get plenty of exercise and vigorous movement to counteract the natural sluggishness of this season. Make time for rejuvenating spring cleanses and purification treatments like Panchakarma.

A Comprehensive Journey into Ayurvedic Healing

As spring turns into summer, Pitta dosha comes into dominance as nature's transformative energies shine brightly. The summer heat stirs up fiery Pitta qualities in the body like hotness, intensity, acidity and sharpness. To balance summer's Pitta influences, Ayurveda suggests drinking cooling herbs like mint, fennel and cilantro, and emphasizing sweet, astringent and bitter foods. Staying hydrated, avoiding excessive outdoor heat, applying cooling oils, and finding relaxation through meditation and spirituality will keep Pitta pacified.

Autumn approaches as Vata dosha takes hold, bringing lightness, dryness, windiness and quickness of change. Our bodies tend to feel scattered and fatigued in fall as Vata increases. Follow an autumn Ayurvedic routine focused on grounding, stability and nourishment. Favor warm, moist, mildly spiced foods like stews, soups and oatmeal. Massaging the body with sesame oil provides needed hydration. Establish regular sleep times and keep up meditation and centering yoga poses.

Finally, chilly Kapha winter emerges, dominated by coldness, heaviness and water. Congestion, weight gain, lethargy and depression can affect those with excess Kapha in winter. Lighten up your diet with warm spices, light grains and plenty of cooked vegetables. Stay active with vigorous exercise that generates inner heat. Schedule treatments like Ayurvedic oil massages, heat therapy and cleansing to prevent Kapha accumulation. Adapt clothing, go to bed early and meditate on warming solar energies.

Ritucharya provides guiding principles for each season, but we are complex beings with unique constitutions. Notice how each season impacts your personal doshas and wellbeing. You may need to emphasize opposite qualities to find balance. Vatas tend to struggle in autumn, Pittas in summer, and Kaphas in winter and spring. Keep adjusting your routines through deeper awareness and experience.

The yearly cycle of seasonal change is plunging into spiritual mystery. Since ancient times, humans have tuned into the wisdom of living harmoniously with seasonal energies. Ritucharya allows us to rediscover our place within the Wheel of the Year and the perpetual cycle of universal consciousness finding balance through nature's cadence. Each phase of the seasonal round offers opportunities for renewal, learning and spiritual growth.

Ayurveda provides instructions for aligning with the seasons, but embodiment and inner wisdom is key. Observe how the qualities of each season affect your body, mind and spirit. Notice where you feel in sync or out of sync. Let nature guide you, use all your senses, and find creative ways to adapt. See each transition as a chance to let go, cleanse and start fresh. Trust your deeper intuition to know what you need in each moment.

The impact of the seasons goes beyond the physical realm. Our moods, emotions and behaviors shift along with changing seasons and doshas. Sadness often emerges in cold, heavy winters. We can feel agitated and angry during intense Pitta summers. Vata autumn stirs up fear and anxiety. Springtime Kapha brings optimism and calm. Ritucharya teaches how to smooth out these seasonal emotional ups and downs.

Nature's seasonal dance is always changing, yet always enduring. Do your best to move gracefully with her rhythms, but don't force. Be patient with yourself as you adapt. Celebrate each phase, finding unique gifts and lessons. Know that all is cyclical - no season lasts forever. Stay centered within your inner light. Then joy, health and soulful living will flower eternally through all of nature's seasons.

4.3 Dinacharya: Morning and Evening Routines

The ancient practice of dinacharya provides guidelines for daily self-care routines to harmonize body, mind and spirit. Dinacharya means "daily conduct" in Sanskrit. These Ayurvedic rituals align us with nature's rhythms, enhance vitality and prevent disease.

The morning dinacharya routine gently awakens our bodies and conscious awareness. Upon rising, take a moment to set a Sankalpa, a positive intention for your day. Next, purify your mouth by scraping your tongue and brushing with herbs like triphala powder to remove ama and energize digestion. Oil pulling is another excellent oral detox technique.

Eliminate waste and refresh your body through natural elimination. Ayurveda traditionally recommends self-massage and dry-brushing before showering to stimulate circulation, remove impurities and absorb oil. Apply a light coating of nourishing oil like coconut, jojoba or almond before bathing.

A warm shower helps energize, or a cool one reduces excess heat. Use only natural cleansers free of chemicals. Scrubbing with a pair of soft gloves helps slough off dead cells. Spend a few minutes meditating under the flowing water.

After bathing, put on clean, comfortable, seasonal clothing and apply essential oils at pulse points to uplift mood. Stretching, yoga or a short walk activates the body's channels and gets energy flowing. Pranayama breathing exercises oxygenate and vitalize. Chanting or journaling also cleanses the mind.

Drink a glass of cool water with lemon to hydrate and awaken digestion. Scrape your tongue again and use oral care herbs. Nasal irrigation with a neti pot clears the sinuses and purifies prana. Oil massage aligns the doshas, nourishes the tissues and enhances health. Do some easy stretches or joint rotations.

Meditate to develop inner stillness before the busy day. Offer gratitude for your blessings. Visualize radiant health and send loving-kindness to all. Chanting mantras like Om generates positivity. Agnihotra and yagya rituals purify the aura through healing fire and mantras.

Eat a light, easy-to-digest breakfast, ideally warm, savory and well-spiced. Never skip the first meal. For Vatas enjoy oatmeal; for Pittas try eggs; for Kaphas have warm cereal. Wait until Agni is robust before larger meals later. Some Ayurvedic texts suggest fasting till lunch.

Your morning routine will evolve and change. Customize it to your needs in each season. The key is starting the day mindfully, cleansing impurities, stimulating digestion and setting healthy intentions. When we align first thing, it ripples through our entire day.

The evening dinacharya mirrors the morning, winding us down into peaceful nighttime rest. As the sun begins lowering, Vata energy accumulates and can make our minds restless. Slow down in the early evening - avoid overstimulating media, heavy food, work or socializing.

Begin transitioning towards introspection. Drink some relaxing herbal tea like chamomile. Gently stretch any tension from your body. Practice restorative yoga poses. Give yourself an oil massage or aromatherapy foot soak.

Spend quality time with loved ones or alone in reflection as night approaches. Write in a journal. Ponder the lessons of your day. Feel gratitude, send forgiveness, let go of what no longer serves you. Chanting and meditation bring equanimity.

Prepare for restful sleep. Turn off electronics. Dim the lights. Set your bedroom temperature a little cool. Apply essential oils to your pulse points. Drink warm milk with spices like turmeric, cinnamon, cardamom and nutmeg.

Before bed, scrape your tongue, swish sesame oil in your mouth and brush gently with a soft toothbrush and powder like clove and neem. Wash your face and remove makeup. Give your body a dry brushing to activate circulation.

Light an oil lamp or candle as you get into bed. Offer a prayer of gratitude for life's blessings. Send loving wishes to those who are struggling and unwell. Visualize absorbing deep, restful sleep. If the mind is active, try meditation. Let go of tomorrow's worries.

The evening routine helps separate our daytime activity from much-needed nightly stillness and restoration. When we consciously transition from Yang to Yin each day, our bodies gracefully move into deep, nourishing sleep. We awaken fresh, vital and ready for a new day.The dinacharya rituals provide an ancient template for self-care and wellbeing. But modern life often prevents us from having enough time for lengthy routines. Adapt dinacharya to your unique needs and schedule, while honoring its wisdom. Even small additions can make a difference.

For busy mornings, try a short meditation, oil massage of face and feet only, tongue scraping, lemon water and breakfast. Save longer practices for days off. On evenings when you're rushed, take five minutes to relax, offer gratitude and set positive intentions for rest.

Integrate mini dinacharya rituals throughout your day. Sip hot water with ginger to kindle your inner fire. Take a few deep breaths before meetings or phone calls. Stretch your neck and shoulders when you've been sitting a while. Sniff an uplifting essential oil when you need a mood boost.

Travel dinacharya helps you stay balanced on trips when routines are disrupted. Pack tongue scraper, essential oils, herbs, green juice powder, neti pot. Wake up early to meditate before a busy day of activities. Unwind in the evenings with journaling and oil massage.

Dinacharya during illness supports the healing process. Get extra rest, drink cleansing kitchari, do gentle oil massage, meditate visualizing recovery. Avoid excess sensory input and distractions. Let your body direct what it needs.

Menstruating women need modified dinacharya aligned with cyclic changes. Emphasize rest, avoid cold, fasting or excess exertion. Follow cravings for wholesome foods. Use heat on the lower abdomen and oil massage. Pamper yourself through this sacred window of inwardness.

During pregnancy, nurture yourself and growing baby through adjusted routines. Include prenatal yoga, swimming, short walks, oil massage on breasts and belly. Meditate connecting to your baby. Eat light, nourishing foods. Rest whenever possible.

Parents can teach children dinacharya from a young age - making health routines fun and engaging. Share Ayurvedic wisdom as kids grow older. Teens especially need supportive dinacharya as hormones fluctuate.

Seniors also thrive with adapted dinacharya for their changing bodies and energies. Focus on relaxation, gentle movement, light diet and herbal support. Stay connected to the community. Include practices like chanting and visualization.

Dinacharya is a highly personal, intuitive ritual. Follow your inner guidance above all. You may be drawn to practice at different times than described. Honor genuine needs like extra sleep or rest. Feel the rhythms of your unique constitution.

Create a dinacharya sanctuary - a peaceful, uncluttered space to ground yourself. Include items that nourish each sense - soft fabrics, essential oils, flowers, candlelight, spiritual art, music. Want inspiration? Study zen home design.

Combine dinacharya with other Ayurvedic routines for amplified benefits. Ritucharya seasonal protocols enhance effects. Follow dinacharya before your sitting meditation. Integrate suitable asanas or pranayama.

Weave in spiritual practices that resonate for you - chanting, heart-centered prayer, singing bowl sound healing, affirmations, gardening, communing with nature. Welcome divinity into your routines.

Check in regularly with your dinacharya. As life evolves, revise routines that no longer fit. Trust your inner wisdom to guide changes. Sometimes less structure is called for. Stay open and aware.

The fruits of dinacharya go far beyond physical health. These rituals cultivate mindfulness, self-compassion and inner peace. Performing dinacharya with awareness transforms it into a moving meditation.

When we infuse consciousness into daily rituals, outer actions become sacred offerings that align us with the cosmic rhythms underlying all life. We touch into the timeless mystery.

Make dinacharya rituals your own, flowing from your heartbeat. No need for rigid schedules or complex steps - simply be in tune with your inner nature. Each moment here is a precious gift. Care for your temporary temple with gentle reverence, remembering always the eternal light within.

4.4 Special Seasonal Routines

In addition to daily dinacharya, Ayurveda provides rejuvenating seasonal rituals to purify the body and amplify vitality at key times of year. These practices enhance the effects of ritucharya seasonal protocols, promoting swastha - optimal health and wellbeing.

The junctions between seasons are important transition points energetically. Nature undergoes transformation between distinctly different periods. Our bodies and minds likewise need cleansing, renewal and preparation for the next seasonal phase.

Spring is dominated by Kapha dosha, the force of growth and nourishment. As cold winter melts into the fertile moisture of spring, Ayurveda recommends panchakarma purification therapies. These eliminate accumulations of toxins, fat and excess Kapha from the winter months. Panchakarma lightens and rejuvenates, enhancing awareness, fitness and the immunity boost spring naturally provides.

Early summer is when we fully transition into Pitta season as temperatures climb and the sun shines strong. Pitta's fiery qualities of heat, oiliness, lightness and sharpness increase in nature. Purification is again recommended through fasting and elimination therapies. These cool down internal heat, reducing excess Pitta before it can accumulate. Light foods, aroma therapy, cold baths and time in nature provide Pitta-soothing relief.

Late summer bridges the movement from Pitta summer into Vata autumn. As heat peaks in August, our bodies and minds are depleted. We crave rest and recovery. Ayurveda recommends relaxation techniques and rejuvenation therapies involving herbally infused oils. These build strength, buffering our nervous systems for Vata season's cold, dryness, unpredictability and chaos.

Fall cleanses rebalance Vata, preventing its qualities of lightness, drying, swiftness and irregularity from excessively building. Food should be warm, heavy and oily. Gentle yoga, meditation and massage calm the nervous system. Warming essential oils protect against fluctuating fall temperatures. Vata-pacifying rituals restore equilibrium before winter.

As the year comes full circle back to Kapha winter, coldness, dullness and heaviness increase. Ayurveda prescribes cleansing fasts, exercise and light, dry, warming, spiced foods. We focus less outward to counter the inward pull of winter. Conserving energy, introspection and meditation allow full gestation of the year's wisdom so we emerge renewed in spring.

While Ayurveda recommends seasonal rejuvenation and cleansing for all, these rituals are especially vital for those with chronic health issues, repeat infections, congestion, neurological imbalance, autoimmunity, obesity, chronic pain, fatigue, insomnia, anxiety, depression or addiction. Periodic purification preemptively prevents disease and decline for those susceptible.

Even in youth with strong immunity and energy, seasonal rituals keep pathogenic forces from slowly accumulating over years into chronic degeneration and dysfunction. They sustain our natural radiance, joyful vitality and peak performance through life's seasons.

Plan your seasonal wellness rituals a month in advance. Do panchakarma under an Ayurvedic physician's guidance. For home practice, choose cleansing strategies within your level of health and comfort - from simple mono-diets or fasting to more intensive eliminative procedures.

Combine physical cleansing with mental purification through prayer, chanting, meditation, pranayama, reflection and spiritual study. Direct focus inward to enhance wisdom, patience, empathy and consciousness. Withdrawing attention from worldly involvement allows our inner being to integrate lessons and visions of the ending season.

Keep a meditation journal to crystallize your insights. Write poetry, make art, play music, spend time in nature - creative activities open inner doors. Dance ecstatically to release stagnation. Share future dreams with loved ones. Chant Om to unite past, present and future in the eternal now.

Rituals work best in community, gathering with others for purification retreats. Prepare special seasonal meals together infused with healing spices, laughter and spiritual communion. Explore local temples, mountains, forests, rivers - places of power to absorb nature's revitalizing prana.

Honoring seasonal wellness traditions aligns us with the profound ebb and flow of the cosmic tides. Through dis-identification with our temporary forms, we remember our unchanging peaceful essence. Seasonal rejuvenation rituals clear space for our universal life force to flow unobstructed.While extensive seasonal rituals provide maximum benefit, any level of observance connects us to nature's cyclical wisdom. Even brief practices enhance awareness of environmental energies and their subtle impact on our bodies and consciousness.

On equinoxes and solstices, wake with the sunrise, meditate outdoors, create small earth altars from natural objects, share seasonal foods with loved ones. Chant Om as you offer flowers, fruits, grains, spices into a fire ceremony of gratitude.

The full and new moons are ideal for cleansing fasts. Drink herbal teas, lemon water or juice as you rest and reflect. Release attachments and stagnation under Luna's illumination. Set intentions for new beginnings. Open to your highest potential.

On lunar and solar eclipses, chant Om during the exact minutes of obscuration to activate ritual power. Donate or release outdated items clearing space for positive change. Meditate on impermanence and life's mysteriously interwoven threads of Karma.

When seasonal allergies arise, do neti sinus rinses for relief and purification. Eat bland, easy to digest meals. Take digestive spices like ginger and fennel which clear ama from micro-channels. Increase immunity with bitter and astringent herbs.

As spring's Kapha wetness induces colds and congestion, fast on warming soups and kitchari. Stay dry, sleep early, and avoid cold dairy. Take steamy diaphoretic herbs to open pores like ginger, black pepper, turmeric. Kapha-reducing rituals restore lightness.

When summer's heat aggravates Pitta sharpness causing rashes or burning indigestion, fast on cooling foods like berries, melons, aloe vera. Bathe in cool water with essential oils. Wear pearls and moonstone. Chant cooling mantras. Meditate on oceans, rivers, rain.

If Vata dryness in fall provokes anxiety, fear or insomnia, self-massage daily with oil. Drink warm milk with spices before bed. Eat plenty of nuts, avocados and hydrating foods. Turn screens off after sunset and read spiritual books.

To prevent Kapha winter lethargy, depression or weight gain, brush skin dry before showering. Take ginger baths,include honey and raw sugar in tea or warm cereal,exercise outdoors during peak daylight,socialize more,keep active and creative.

In heat waves, stay cool indoors, eat cucumbers, coconut water, and mint. Gentle yoga loosens heat from tissues. Pearl powder masks soothe fiery skin. Sandalwood, rose, lavender essential oils calm overloaded Pittas.

When harsh winter weather aggravates Vata, bundle up warmly. Keep feet covered and head protected. Eat oil-rich soups and stews. Take Ashwagandha to steady nerves. Keep active with gentle indoor exercise. Move slowly and meditate often.

With conscious attention, we can creatively adapt Ayurveda's profound seasonal wisdom into our fast-paced modern lives. Intention and awareness are key. Engaging ritual taps into cosmic energies beyond the physical. Even small adjustments open subtle energetic portals, initiating transformations of body, mind and soul.

While dinacharya and ritucharya establish foundational routines, listen within for inner guidance on foods, activities, meditations, and practices uniquely suited to balance your individual constitution in each season. Follow personalized inspirations - your path arises from inner truth.

Ayurveda reminds us of our place within nature's eternal seasonal flow. Riding Her cycles, we learn profound patience, faith and surrender. We are humble students sitting in Her lap, growing wise through lessons of impermanence, detachment and renewal.

Aligning efforts with universal currents saves energy. Move with the cosmic tides - not against them. Balance is organic, not forced. We receive support, grace and strength to overcome obstacles. Like mighty rivers carving through rock, nature's currents smoothen out rough edges if we move in harmony.

Beyond rituals, meditate simply on the beauty of each transitory season. Marvel at how life adapts to sun and rain. Be present with bare winter trees and budding sprouts alike. Open fully to all textures life offers. Equanimity and joy naturally follow.

The Earth keeps dancing, never tiring as She endlessly pirouettes through phases. To dance in flow with Great Nature is to let go of struggles and move as waves returning to a timeless sea of blissful eternal being.

4.5 Integrating Ayurvedic Routines

Ayurveda provides an intricate web of daily and seasonal routines for optimal health. While powerful practices, these protocols take dedication to fully integrate into busy modern lifestyles. With wisdom and adaptability, we can incorporate Ayurvedic wisdom into everyday living.

It is wise to focus first on consistency with basic rituals over trying to achieve perfection or complexity right away. Just wake up on time each morning for your adapted routine. Go to bed before 10pm every night. Eat your main meal at noon. Simple rhythms like these establish momentum that unfolds into deeper wisdom over time.

When first starting out, choose dinacharya protocols you feel most inspired by to integrate - whether tongue scraping, dry brushing, self-massage, meditation, yoga or nourishing breakfast rituals. Select those practices that feel integrative and nourishing for your unique mind-body constitution. The positive results you experience will motivate you to gradually expand your routines.

Rather than over-stretching your capacity too quickly, it is skillful to set gradual goals at first like "meditate 5 minutes daily this month." Then you can slowly increase your time or practice as inner stamina develops. Be as gentle with yourself as if you were training for a marathon. Consistency develops greater inner capacity much more than sporadic intensity.

It helps immensely to schedule set ritual times into your calendar as non-negotiable appointments, just like you would do important work meetings or doctor visits. Mark out consistent times so the practices become embedded as habits. But also allow flexibility when emergencies come up – don't become rigidly attached to perfection.

Keep in mind that rituals need not be lengthy to provide transformative benefits. Even just 5 minutes of oil massage, pranayama, meditation or journaling can shift nervous system balance and promote self-awareness in powerful ways. Even short practices will sow seeds of wellbeing that blossom over time.

Take some time to identify the optimal times to engage your rituals that align with your natural bio-cycles. Are you a morning person suited to rise early? Or a night owl who needs evening rituals? Craft your routines to fit with your individual flow.

For busy weekdays, streamline morning routines to the essentials, saving more extensive rejuvenating practices for leisurely weekends when you have spacious time to unwind deeply. Completely replenish your spirit in the evenings after work – transition smoothly into rest.

You can also integrate mini-rituals throughout busy days – pause to breathe consciously, offer gratitude, repeat a mantra, visualize goals, stretch your body, and consume herbal tea mindfully. Just a few minutes of ritual here and there provides benefits.

If you miss your full routine occasionally due to work obligations or family needs, simply get back to it the next day without self-judgment. Beating yourself up emotionally breaks momentum much more severely than sporadic lapses do. Forgive yourself, course correct gently, and carry on.

During times of increased worldly obligations – holiday travel, family demands, work deadlines or illness recovery – adapt and simplify your practices to what is absolutely nourishing and integrative for you in the moment. Keep things simple but wise. Then return fully to your normal routines when duties pass.It is insightful to identify obstacles that commonly sabotage consistency with rituals – lack of preparation/planning, inadequate motivation, insufficient sleep, high stress, negative attitude, perfectionistic standards. Then proactively work to creatively resolve what undermines your commitment.

If you lose inspiration halfway into establishing new rituals, carefully pinpoint what specific practices felt too difficult to sustain long-term. Then thoughtfully adjust and simplify those challenging areas first before attempting to add any further protocols. Go step by step.

Cultivating "ritual allies" can greatly uplift energy and commitment – participating in motivating community classes, working with a health coach, doing practices together with friends, joining a spiritual community. Share goals, give reminders, schedule meet-ups. Social support sustains inspiration to grow rituals.

When establishing family routines, have reasonable expectations about children's ability to participate based on their ages, temperaments and energy levels. Make rituals fun through songs, stories, engaging games. Nurture their natural enthusiasm rather than force. Lead by your own example.

Ayurvedic rituals will naturally wax and wane like the flowing seasons and cycles of life. Learn to flow with your changing inner capacity for structure. Pushing too hard typically leads to burnout. Find balance between effort and rest. Trust your deeper intuitive rhythms.

Rituals are highly personal, intuitive arts. Follow your own inner guidance on appropriate practices above all, even if advice suggests otherwise. You may be drawn to engage in rituals at different times than described in textbooks. Honor your unique biological needs.

Create a soothing "ritual sanctuary" – a clutter-free, peaceful space to ground yourself in practices. Include items that nourish all senses – soft fabrics, essential oils, flowers, candlelight, inspiriting artwork, sacred music. Study zen home design for inspiration.

Combine dinacharya and ritucharya with other complementary Ayurvedic routines for amplified benefits. For example, integrate suitable yoga asanas and pranayama breathing exercises. Or follow dinacharya before your sitting meditation routine.

Weave in spiritual practices that most resonate – chanting, heart-centered prayer, singing bowl sound healing, affirmations, gardening, communing with nature. Welcome divinity and higher wisdom into the rituals.

Check in regularly with yourself on the appropriateness of your routines. As your life situation evolves, mindfully revise practices that no longer fit. Trust inner wisdom to guide timing and types of supportive changes. Stay open and aware.

The fruits gained from Ayurvedic rituals extend far beyond physical health and wellbeing. These practices also cultivate mindfulness, self-compassion and inner peace. Performing them with full awareness transforms routines into moving meditations.

When we infuse consciousness into daily rituals, outer actions become sacred offerings aligning us with the benevolent cosmic rhythms underlying all life. We touch the timeless mystery.

Make rituals your own unique expression flowing from your inner truth. No need for rigid schedules or complex steps – simply attune to natural wisdom, caring for your temporary temple with gentle reverence while remembering the eternal light within.

4.6 Overcoming Obstacles to Routines

Ayurvedic routines provide a blueprint for optimal health and wellbeing. Yet despite their benefits, many find dinacharya and ritucharya protocols challenging to implement fully into the chaos of modern life. With self-compassion, creativity and patience, we can overcome common obstacles blocking our ritual practice.

Lack of time is the biggest barrier faced, as most are overbooked juggling work, family, social demands and chores.strategically integrating mini-rituals throughout the day helps. Even five minutes of oil massage, stretching, meditation or nature break will center and nourish. Schedule priorities, trim activities that deplete.

Insufficient motivation and consistency is common, as new habits require effort before becoming automatic. Start with small attainable steps. Schedule rituals to build momentum. Cultivate curiosity in their effects. Find an accountability partner. Reward milestones. Your inspiration will grow as benefits unfold.

Many struggle with early morning wake-up times prescribed in dinacharya, especially if constitutionally a night owl. Be compassionate with bio-rhythms. Retire early to rest fully rather than force rising, meditating when exhausted. Focus on sleep hygiene first.

Difficulty calming the restless distractible mind presents an obstacle for meditation, breathwork and other centering practices. Approach with patience and keep trying brief sessions. Explore different techniques. Use guided meditations initially. Develop concentration gradually.

Physical or emotional pain can impede the mindfulness demanded in rituals. When suffering, focus on soothing, grounding activities or loving connection. Seek healing first before introducing more discipline. Honor your needs.

Some lack comprehension of Ayurvedic wisdom required for nuanced practices. Study digestible resources, consult teachers and keep learning through experience. Wisdom unfolds step by step. Stay open to make course corrections.

Perfectionistic standards hinder consistency, as we deem efforts don't measure up. Focus on progress, not immediate mastery. Keep refining through self-study and support. Skill develops over time. Remember to enjoy your unique journey.

Limited belief in rituals creates doubt and low motivation. Observe tangible benefits with an open mind. Consider the power of intention. Research epigenetics. Start with secular practices before adding spiritual rituals only if called. Build faith slowly.

Cluttered, chaotic spaces prevent creating a ritual sanctuary. Minimize possessions, organize items, designate peaceful corners. Display spiritual art, soft lighting, green plants and flowers. Clear energy with sound, herbs, crystals. Make your altar cozy.

Some struggle with dietary changes, tastes and prep time. Gradually introduce new foods or spices. Seek easy plant-based recipes. Batch cook or use a meal service initially. Make eating the proper diet an enjoyable ritual itself.

Financial constraints limit access to costly treatments, supplements or organic foods. Explore low cost options like meditation, yoga, walks and food co-ops. Reconsider priorities, reduce expenses draining health. Creativity overcomes lack of funds.

Certain family or social dynamics resist implementing rituals, deliberately or unintentionally. Lovingly communicate benefits and set boundaries. Offer to include them. Seek tribes who uplift your journey, while also being respectful.

With perseverance and adaptation, almost all obstacles blocking ritual practice can be smoothed. Establish the right intention, take small steps, and celebrate your progress. Each effort refines wisdom, even if practices evolve over time. Consistency is key.While establishing optimal rituals takes effort initially, the most powerful step is simply beginning – taking that first small action. When we engage with intention and consistency, inner wisdom unfolds organically to refine practices and overcome obstacles in time.

Have compassion for where you are now, while holding a vision of your highest potential. See every effort as progress, without being attached to specific outcomes. Trust Ayurveda's timeless principles to bear fruits ripened in the proper season.

We all face challenges and limitations of body, mind, resources or circumstances. Yet even from our unique starting points, we can chart a path towards greater balance and inner peace. Possibilities abound within most situations through creativity.

Reflect on why you were originally drawn to Ayurveda. Reconnecting to your core inspiration provides motivation, especially when you meet hurdles. Your sincerity will carry you through temporary setbacks.

When rituals feel challenging, pare back to the most essential nourishing practices that make you feel grounded and integrated. Then slowly build again from that foundation when you're ready for more discipline.

Be mindful of taking on too much too fast in your enthusiasm. Going all-in immediately can burn out passion. Add incremental steps gradually after establishing a new baseline. Consistency generates momentum.

Accept natural ebbs and flows in your capacity for spiritual disciplines. We all have busy and quiet seasons. Meditate, fast and practice silence during retreats. Focus on restorative rituals during hectic periods.

Consider keeping a ritual journal to integrate lessons, reflect on progress and clarify appropriate practices as life evolves. Writing integrates wisdom into consciousness and intention into manifestation.

Rituals potentiate each other's effects when performed in sequence. For example, yoga and meditation have a deeper impact when following tongue scraping, oil massage and hot shower. Explore skillful combinations.

Creating optimal health requires honoring all facets of life – not just spiritual development, but also relationships, career, creative expression, financial independence, and life purpose. Integrate all in the right balance.

Be wary of excessive sternness or austerity in rituals. While disciplines have value, avoid rigidity, self-judgment or pushing beyond capacity. Nourish yourself with self-love and compassion.

Patience and perseverance are paramount. With time and grace, nearly all obstacles to ritual practice can be overcome. What matters most is your sincere intention to walk an Ayurvedic path, starting right where you are.

Consistency in small steps leads to giant leaps. Keep refining practices without expecting perfection. Progress will come through compassionate awareness, effort and wisdom accrued from experience. Your steady devotion sows blessings.

Chapter 5

The Purifying Power of Panchakarma

5.1 Understanding the Panchakarma Purification Process

Panchakarma is Ayurveda's time-tested detoxification protocol for cleansing accumulated wastes and toxins while rejuvenating the body, mind and consciousness. The term "panchakarma" means five main actions in Sanskrit – these cleansing techniques restore harmonic balance to the doshas, dhatus and malas.

Ayurveda recognizes we regularly accumulate physical and emotional toxins from poor diet, negative emotions, repressed trauma, environmental pollutants and daily metabolic byproducts. Imbibed toxins that cannot be eliminated become lodged and clog subtle channels and tissues, impairing cellular nutrition. This accumulation of undigested matter is called "ama."

Ama obstructs free flow of prana, lymphatic fluids and blood, causing disorder to manifest in the body and mind over time. Panchakarma reverses this pathogenic process through calculated cleansing of accumulated wastes at their precise sites of origin and deposition.

The purifying actions of Panchakarma flush ama out of deep tissues, the digestive tract, lungs and sinuses, where they lodge and perpetuate disease. After purification, fresh nutrients and prana can again nourish the body as doshas regain equilibrium.

A Comprehensive Journey into Ayurvedic Healing

Panchakarma employs five main actions to cleanse the body holistically. Nasal administration of medicated oils clears accumulated wastes from the nostrils, sinuses and upper respiratory tract. Therapeutic vomiting eliminates excesses from kapha areas. Purgation through ingesting laxative substances expels impurities from pitta regions. Medicated oil enemas remove toxins from vata zones. And decoction enemas flush wastes from the intestinal tract.

In addition, Ayurveda uses supporting procedures like therapeutic massage, steam, specialized diet, herbs, sound therapy and yoga postures to assist the comprehensive cleansing process. All practices are administered at the junctions between seasons for maximum purification benefits.

Specially prepared herbalized oils and ghees lubricate and loosen toxins from tissues. Therapeutic vomiting and purgation then expel these loosened impurities from kapha sites. Medicated oil and decoction enemas remove excess doshas and wastes from pitta and vata areas. Nasal cleansing clears residues from the nasal passages and upper respiratory tract.

This systematic purification of every bodily system rejuvenates all organ networks together. Toxins lodged deeply in dhatus, srotas and malas are effectively cleansed from their precise sites of origin. This comprehensive bio cleansing resets the body's innate self-healing intelligence.

The cleansing is followed by herbal tonics and a health-promoting diet to rebuild tissue and restore the digestive fire. As ama is fully cleared from the physiology, the unobstructed flow of prana profoundly nourishes body, mind and spirit. The mind becomes lucid, calm and sattvic.

Panchakarma is Ayurveda's ultimate mind-body healing modality, skillfully prescribed to treat almost every disorder when performed properly. But beyond its potent therapeutic effects, Panchakarma frees awareness, expels negativity and opens spiritual channels as steps to Self Realization.While modern detoxification programs focus on cleansing a single system, Ayurveda's Panchakarma protocol works holistically to clear impurities from every bodily tissue simultaneously. This comprehensive biopurification provides deeper and more lasting benefits than partial cleanses.

Panchakarma's systematic elimination of deep-rooted toxins resets the physiology to its natural state of balance, supporting the body's innate wisdom to heal and thrive. As ama is cleared and agni strengthened, we embody greater vitality on physical, mental and spiritual levels.

When performed properly by an experienced practitioner, Panchakarma treatments are safe, effective and gentle. Side effects are rare, although temporary fatigue, headache or loose stools can sometimes occur as toxins are loosened. Experienced practitioners will skillfully minimize reactions.

Panchakarma is prescribed therapeutically for almost every imbalance and disease in the Ayurvedic canon, from gastrointestinal issues to diabetes, autoimmunity, musculoskeletal problems, depression, anxiety, skin conditions, gynecological disorders, infertility, neurological conditions and more.

Clinical results show profound healing in those who undergo comprehensive Panchakarma treatment. Studies document reduced arthritis pain, stabilized blood sugar, lower cholesterol and lipids, improved immunity, detoxification of heavy metals and environmental chemicals, enhanced fertility, mental clarity and inner peace.

While Panchakarma originated centuries ago, modern scientific analysis now validates its efficacy. Clinical research affirms the antioxidant, anti-inflammatory, neuroprotective, cardio-protective, anti-diabetic, anti-anxiety, antidepressant and detoxifying actions of key Panchakarma herbs.

However, cleansing alone cannot guarantee lasting wellness. Lifestyle habits must align with individual constitution to sustain balance after Panchakarma. The practitioner customizes guidance on ideal diet, activities, routines and inner work to integrate Ayurveda fully into daily life.

Panchakarma cleanses both physiological and psychological toxins that distort the mind and veil consciousness. As clarity expands, we gain profound insights into unhealthy patterns that perpetuate suffering. These realizations empower us to let go and make conscious choices supporting lasting inner freedom.

Beyond curing diseases, Panchakarma's deepest benefit is awakening spiritual awareness. Removing vitiated doshas and toxins opens channels for higher perception and direct experience of unity. Purification illuminates the pure joy, peace and divinity innate to our core being.

While intensive programs are most transformative, even lighter versions of Panchakarma provide deep cleansing and renewal. under an Ayurvedic physician's supervision, one can safely explore their optimal level of purification. This wisdom tradition guides us to embody our highest vitality in every sense.

Through Panchakarma, Ayurveda delivers its ultimate promise - complete mind-body purification and rejuvenation. By dissolving all toxins and imbalances at their root, this classical panacea restores wholeness on all levels of existence. The timeless science of life awakens our full potential for radiant health, inner peace and Self-realization.

5.2 Preparing for Panchakarma

Panchakarma requires proper preparation to cleanse the body safely and effectively. Pre-purification steps liquefy and guide toxins into the gastrointestinal tract for elimination. An experienced Ayurvedic doctor skillfully oversees preparation based on your unique health profile.

Pre-panchakarma care typically begins one month before intensive treatment. Your practitioner will prescribe dietary adjustments and herbs to pacify imbalanced doshas and kindle agni. Light, easy-to-digest foods cleanse the GI tract. Ghee in particular lubricates for the elimination of toxins.

You may be directed to gradually decrease intake of heavy foods, dairy, raw vegetables, fruits, cold drinks, iced water and toxic substances like alcohol, tobacco and non-prescription drugs. It is also beneficial to minimize sensory input through loud music, television, social media and news.

Daily self-massage with warmed Ayurvedic oils helps the body start releasing toxins for elimination. Gentle exercise, yoga, pranayama, meditation and spiritual reflection also prepare the mind and consciousness for optimal purification.

Panchakarma is best undergone at the junction between two seasons when environmental energies assist purification. The body's natural inclination to cleanse itself aligns with enhanced effects of procedures. Spring and fall are ideal times, when kapha and vata accumulate.

A key pre-panchakarma substance is triphala, a classic Ayurvedic formula with three potent dried fruits - haritaki, bibhitaki and amalaki. Triphala's combination of tastes clears toxins without irritation. Take as directed by your practitioner.

A Comprehensive Journey into Ayurvedic Healing

You may be prescribed other purification herbs like dandelion, fennel, ginger, manjishtha, guduchi, turmeric, aloe vera, neem or burdock root. These time-tested botanicals gently flush toxins from organs and tissues.

In addition to preliminary cleansing, proper mindset and environment set you up for a successful process. Take time away from routines and responsibilities. Leave behind stressors, limit digital media. Allow your system to fully rest.

Consider undergoing treatment near a serene natural setting that supports the healing journey. Establish a calm, meditative, inward daily rhythm. Conserve energy for self-care practices and rest. Simplify activities.

Trust in the ancient wisdom of Panchakarma. Let go of desired outcomes. Set your highest intention for purification and awakening, then surrender and observe without judgment as your consciousness is cleansed.

Preliminary cleansing before Panchakarma is a vital phase requiring care and awareness. With proper preparation guided by an expert, the deep-rooted impurities you are ready to release will empty safely, opening space for renewed health and inner growth.During pre-purification, carefully notice how your body and mind respond to the cleansing process. Keep a journal to record insights and any reactions. Stay hydrated, get plenty of rest and contact your practitioner with concerns.

You may experience temporary fatigue, headaches, congestion, heightened emotions, muscle or joint pain as toxins begin releasing. These are normal detoxification symptoms that show purification is occurring. Practices like meditation, massage and rest will alleviate discomfort.

Some people underground panchakarma alone in silence and introspection. For others, undertaking cleansing surrounded by loved ones provides comfort and support. Follow your own needs - there are benefits in both approaches when aligned with intention.

Allow suppressed thoughts, feelings and traumas to surface for resolution and release. Your practitioner will guide you in releasing mental, emotional and psychic toxins as well as physical impurities.

Notice where you hold tension in your body and consciously relax those areas through awareness. Deeply ingrained stress patterns can manifest when purification stirs previously buried energies. Breathe into tight spaces to surrender.

As old layers peel back, you may re-experience past pain or memories. But with faith and courage, this unraveling allows you to finally let go and step forward unburdened. What is liberated through your inner work can never imprison you again.

During preparatory cleansing, introspection and dreamwork provide further opportunities to liberate mental obscurations and karmic imprints. The Coming to Peace process can powerfully digest emotional toxins. Counseling supports mental purification.

Your practitioner will assess if you have adequately prepared for full Panchakarma cleansing, or if more time is needed. When your agni and elimination channels are ready, you can proceed into the intensive treatment phase with confidence.

The preparatory period varies from a few weeks to several months depending on your current health. Be patient with your unique process. Consistency with herbs, diet and rituals gradually cleanses blockages at deeper levels with each cycle.

Remember – discomfort during preparation is temporary, while the revitalized health and inner freedom you gain from proper cleansing is priceless. Continue pacifying your dominant doshas through the ups and downs. The rewards are well worth perseverance.

With expert guidance, earnest inner work and consistent home rituals, your body, mind and spirit will cleanse, align and awaken. Let go of what no longer serves you. Empty and purify yourself completely to receive Panchakarma's profound benefits. A new incarnation of health and inner light awaits you.

5.3 Main Purification Therapies

Panchakarma employs five main purification therapies to eliminate toxins and restore balance in the body and mind. These therapies are expertly administered by trained practitioners after proper preparation. The five therapies work synergistically to address imbalances at deeper levels.

Vamana, also known as emesis therapy, uses specific herbs and processes to induce therapeutic vomiting. It gently clears the upper gastrointestinal tract of kapha imbalances that manifest as excess mucus, congestion, and inflammation. The therapy begins with ingesting vamana dravyas, herbs that loosen kapha and start the vomiting reflex. These are typically taken for a few days along with a strict kapha-reducing diet and other preparatory steps.

On the day of treatment, the practitioner administers more emesis herbs and a medicated steam treatment to further loosen mucus and start the vomiting process. The patient then ingests a large quantity of lukewarm saline water which triggers the urge to vomit. The treatment is complete when a deep clearance of kapha is achieved. Afterwards, the patient rests and continues to follow specific guidelines to allow the body to stabilize.

Vamana is particularly useful for addressing obstinate kapha issues affecting the lungs, sinuses, stomach, and liver. It also helps with skin diseases, asthma, diabetes, and chronic allergies. However, those with heart disease, ulcerative colitis, hernia, or retinal issues should avoid this therapy. When administered properly at appropriate times, vamana provides deep detoxification without depleting the body.

Virechana cleanses the digestive tract through the use of herbs and foods that stimulate bowel movements. This clears pitta and kapha excesses from the small and large intestines, along with toxins, waste byproducts, and excess fat. The goal is to remove deep-seated impurities while upholding proper intestinal function.

Purgation therapy starts with ingesting virechana dravyas, or herbs with a downward flowing action, for several days. Triphala and trivrit are commonly used as they gently stimulate peristalsis. This is accompanied by an easy-to-digest diet to prepare the gut. On the day of treatment, ingestion of more powerful purgatives like castor oil induces multiple bowel movements to fully clear the digestive tract. Afterwards, light meals are consumed and rest is emphasized.

Virechana benefits from many conditions including chronic fever, hyperacidity, bloating, jaundice, gallbladder issues, and hemorrhoids. However, those with ulcerative colitis, diverticulitis, or rectal bleeding should avoid this therapy unless directed by an expert. For most people, virechana with proper preparatory steps poses minimal risks and provides a deep detoxifying effect.

Basti is a therapeutic enema that infuses medicated substances into the colon to balance vata and remove toxins. It is considered the most effective treatment for pacifying vata and restoring harmony in the large intestine. There are two main types: anuvasana basti which uses oil, and niruha basti which uses herbal decoctions.

Anuvasana basti introduces medicated sesame oil or ghee into the rectum which gets absorbed by intestinal walls. This soothes dryness, promotes peristalsis, and relieves constipation. Oil enemas are given routinely to curb vata and are recommended before starting any cleansing routine. Niruha basti contains purifying herbal formulas like dashamoola decoction which wash the rectal walls when held for a short duration. This combats intestinal inflammation and cleans the colon of ama while balancing intestinal flora.

The basti treatment begins with an oil enema which is retained for a specified time before release. This is followed by the herbal retention enema. The entire treatment takes about one hour and is administered two to three times per week. Basti is helpful for multiple conditions including neurological issues, paralysis, waist pain, kidney stones, infertility, and autoimmune disorders. However, care should be taken for those with enlarged prostate issues or recent abdominal surgery. Overall, basti offers a deeply soothing and balancing effect on vata imbalances.

Nasya involves introducing medicated liquids and powders into the nasal passages. This clears excess kapha while eliminating toxins and balancing prana. Regular nasya is beneficial before and after the main purifying therapies.

For the treatment, the practitioner administers a gentle stream of warm ghee, oil, juice, or herbal decoction into each nostril. This helps liquefy mucus so it drains out freely. Afterwards, inhalation of medicated smoke, powders, or vapors provides further cleansing. Herbs like calamus, eucalyptus, peppermint, and ginger root clear the sinus passages and nasal cavities of toxins while increasing circulation.

Nasya alleviates kapha disorders affecting the head and neck including chronic sinusitis, headaches, migraine, and respiratory issues. It improves immunity, lymphatic drainage, and mental clarity while soothing vata-related anxiety and insomnia. Those with acute bleeding, infection, or rhinitis should avoid the therapy until the issues resolve. When done regularly, nasya rejuvenates the entire face, nose, throat, and head region.

Raktamokshana is a traditional detoxifying treatment that removes a small amount of blood from the body. This is an effective option for pitta imbalances involving excess heat in the blood, although the therapy should be supervised by an expert practitioner. Bloodletting helps drain toxins, chemicals, infections, and excess pitta dosha that may have built up in the circulatory system.

There are a few different methods used for raktamokshana. The simplest involves creating small superficial scratches on the skin using a sterile lancet. Blood is allowed to ooze out gently and get absorbed by a cotton pad. Applying antiseptic and a bandage completes the treatment. More involved methods include the use of leech therapy and cupping to draw blood to the surface of the skin. Proper aftercare is taken to avoid infection.

This therapy benefits skin conditions like acne, eczema, and urticaria. It also helps manage pituitary disorders, gout, early stages of cancer, and sudden inflammation in joints or organs. However, those with anemia, bleeding issues, or cardiovascular disease should avoid raktamokshana. When applied judiciously, bloodletting provides a targeted physical cleansing from excess pitta.

The purifying actions of these five therapies eliminate toxins and excesses at deeper levels while restoring balance between vata, pitta, and kapha. Although intense, Panchakarma provides a profound cleansing effect when administered with proper preparatory and post-therapy care under the guidance of a trained Ayurvedic practitioner. The therapies work holistically to renew health and wellbeing in body, mind, and spirit.Panchakarma provides a profound cleansing of body, mind and spirit when administered by a skilled practitioner under proper protocols. However, there are also some supportive therapies that can be safely incorporated at home with guidance. Gentle home therapies like abhyanga massage, nasya, steam inhalation, herbal teas, tongue scraping and castor oil packs help remove superficial toxins while calming the mind and body. They serve as useful preparatory steps before deeper cleansing.

Daily self-massage with cooling coconut oil for pitta, warming sesame for vata, or dry massage for kapha deeply nourishes tissues while stimulating lymphatic drainage. After oil massage, bathing effectively removes surface oil and toxins. Placing a few drops of ghee or oil in each nostril first thing in the morning clears sinus congestion by flushing out impurities. Steam inhalation with eucalyptus, mint and respiratory herbs liquefies mucus so it can drain freely when inhaled over a pot of boiled water. Drinking lighter, astringent herbal teas like cinnamon-ginger for kapha or warming cumin-fennel for vata between meals aids digestion and bile flow to gently cleanse the GI tract. Scraping off bacteria, toxins and dead cells from the tongue surface freshens the breath while supporting the body's detox mechanisms. Applying castor oil packs over the abdomen for 30 minutes before bed improves lymphatic drainage and elimination in the gut. Relaxing in an Epsom salt bath allows magnesium to be absorbed through skin to facilitate cellular detoxification.

When done properly at home on a routine basis, these therapies reduce inflammation, decrease toxic buildup and optimize wellness. However, undergoing the intensive clinical treatments of Panchakarma requires selecting an expert practitioner thoroughly trained in assessment, preparation, safe administration and post-cleanse protocols. Finding a qualified professional certified in the specialized field of Panchakarma ensures appropriate therapies are administered for maximum cleansing benefits and proper aftercare guidance is provided. It is ideal to look for formal Panchakarma certification beyond general Ayurvedic education and several years of experience administering full-scope protocols. Checking credentials from reputable Ayurvedic colleges, affiliations with professional associations, and comfort level during consultations gives reassurance that therapeutic goals will be holistically supported before, during and after treatment.

The powerful internal shifts facilitated through proper Panchakarma treatment should be integrated gradually under practitioner guidance. As energy returns, light easy-to-digest warm and unctuous foods help stoke agni until digestion fully rekindles. Gentle reopening to heavier foods, exercise, work and life routines prevents overexertion. Most importantly, Panchakarma provides motivation to implement positive lifestyle changes supporting health goals. Setting intentions to regularly care for your body, mind and spirit after cleansing allows the benefits to endure and progress.

5.4 Panchakarma at Home

While Panchakarma's intensive clinical treatments require an expert practitioner, there are also some gentle home therapies that can be supportive when done carefully under guidance. Daily oil self-massage, nasya, steam inhalation, herbal teas, tongue scraping and castor oil packs help remove superficial toxins while calming the mind and body in preparation for deeper cleansing. Coconut oil cools pitta, sesame warms vata, and dry massage pacifies kapha when rubbed into tissues before bathing to drain toxins. Drops of ghee or oil in the nostrils first thing in the morning clear impurities trapped overnight. Steaming the face over aromatic herbs liquefies sinus congestion for drainage. Drinking astringent cinnamon-ginger or warming cumin-fennel tea between meals stimulates bile flow for gentle intestinal detox. Scraping the tongue freshens breath by removing accumulated bacteria, toxins and dead cells. Castor oil packs improve lymphatic drainage when applied to the abdomen before bedtime. Absorbing magnesium from a warm Epsom salt bath facilitates relaxation and cellular detox.

When incorporated routinely, these simple home therapies reduce inflammatory toxins and optimize wellness. However, undergoing the intensive clinical processes of Panchakarma requires selecting an expert practitioner thoroughly trained in assessment, preparation, safe administration of treatments and post-cleanse protocols beyond basic Ayurvedic education. Finding a professional certified specifically in Panchakarma, rather than general spa-style treatments, ensures therapies are administered for maximum cleansing benefits within holistic protocols supporting the entire process. Checking credentials from reputable Ayurvedic colleges, years of hands-on experience under guidance, affiliations with professional associations and comfort level during consultations gives confidence that therapeutic goals will be met. Being open to reputable treatment centers or retreats provides immersive healing in a supportive environment. Taking time to find an authentic practitioner guiding you through profound rejuvenation allows Panchakarma's benefits to integrate for lasting wellness.The benefits of Panchakarma continue long after treatment through proper aftercare and long-term lifestyle adjustments. Follow your practitioner's specific recommendations for post-cleanse rest, light diet, and rejuvenation to allow the deep cellular changes to integrate. Gradually resume exercise and regular routines but avoid overexertion. Warm oil massage, meditation, and pranayama help calm the body.

Continue to eat light, easy-to-digest meals favoring warm, unctuous foods as the digestive fire slowly increases. Gradually reintroduce dairy, raw foods, and heavier grains over days to weeks per practitioner guidance. Minimize cold, dry, frozen or reheated foods that suppress agni. Give the body time to recover its full vitality.

Make meditation, breathwork, and self-massage regular habits to release stress and nourish yourself daily. Observe your prakruti and vikruti to choose foods, herbs, aromas, colors, and sounds that balance your mind-body constitution. Keep your mind positive and focused through cleansing cycles. This strengthens ojas to prevent reaccumulation of toxins.

Most importantly, reflect on the internal shifts facilitated by Panchakarma. What physical, mental, and emotional patterns are ready for change? Set intentions going forward to cultivate new positive habits supporting your long-term health goals. Panchakarma provides an opportunity for rebirth into greater harmony and vibrant wellbeing. Allow it to instill renewed motivation to care for your body as the temple of your soul.

Many people find undertaking Panchakarma treatment in a retreat setting away from daily stresses and routine greatly enhances the experience and benefits. Retreats offer a nurturing environment for deep cleansing surrounded by nature and community support. They provide:

Focused Healing: Retreats allow singular focus on healing without distractions. The tranquility facilitates internal awareness and transformation. Therapies, yoga, meditation, and nature instill deep relaxation.

Community Support: Sharing the experience with like-minded people provides encouragement and accountability. Group activities build bonds fostering a spirit of camaraderie.

Holistic Lifestyle: Nutritious Ayurvedic meals, herbal teas, meditation, breathwork, and yoga are built into the daily routine immersing you into the Ayurvedic lifestyle. This empowers integration after returning home.

A Comprehensive Journey into Ayurvedic Healing

Natural Settings: Retreat centers are often situated in serene natural locations like mountains, forests, springs or beaches that are intrinsically calming and energizing. Nature enhances wellbeing.

Customized Protocols: Experienced specialists design personalized therapy programs to specifically address your current health status and concerns. Customization improves outcomes.

While Panchakarma programs are available locally in some urban areas, traveling to reputable retreats in India or Western centers of Ayurvedic excellence allows deep immersion into transformative therapies within a synergistic healing milieu. Many find this intensive process easier to embrace by stepping away from everyday environments and responsibilities for a time. Investing this focus encourages positive growth and renewed perspective.

If undertaking Panchakarma treatment near home without the retreat format, be sure to create space for quietude, reflection and integration of the changes facilitated. Have simplicity, leisurely pacing and warmth surround you while giving your body-mind time and care to realign after the deep cleansing process. Let go of clutter and busyness as much as possible to allow the therapy's benefits to gently permeate your being.

Whether in a formal retreat setting or not, Panchakarma provides a valuable chance to renew, gain wisdom about your inner workings, and realign with your highest self. Approaching this therapy with openness and positivity allows it to work its magic, while integration afterwards continues the transformation through positive changes, uplifted state of mind, and focus on overall wellbeing."

5.5 Finding a Panchakarma Practitioner

Undergoing Panchakarma therapy requires finding an experienced practitioner thoroughly trained beyond basic Ayurvedic education in assessment, preparation, administration of treatments, and post-cleanse care. Their specialty Panchakarma certification through reputable institutions signifies mastery of the comprehensive cleansing methodologies, not just general spa-style treatments. Hands-on expertise administering intensive protocols under seasoned mentorship confers practical skills and clinical wisdom. Holistic preparatory and restorative techniques should surround the main therapies to support the entire mind-body-spirit process. Formal Ayurvedic education and credentials from respected colleges provide a solid foundation. Affiliations with professional associations upholding rigorous standards encourage excellence through accountability. Scheduling an introductory consultation, whether by phone or in-person, allows you to assess comfort level and customization of treatments for your needs. Since Panchakarma excellence can be concentrated in certain geographic areas, consider traveling to a reputable center or immersive retreat if options near home seem inadequate. Taking time to find an authentic practitioner well-matched to guide your profound cleansing journey is essential.

Speaking to prospective practitioners during initial consultations reveals their approach, competence and practice style to inform your decision. Ask how long they have focused on Panchakarma specifically and the nature of their training for firsthand mastery. Inquire about their certification process through accredited institutes. Determine if they personalize therapy choices through careful assessment versus taking a "one-size-fits-all" approach. Ask about preparatory and restorative protocols surrounding treatments for holistic support. Seek ongoing follow up care and longitudinal guidance to optimize integration. Have them describe a typical retreat or treatment program to ensure comfortable components. Verify attentive safety monitoring and skill managing cleansing reactions. Consider specialties relevant to your health concerns. While Panchakarma expertise is key, also look for foundational Ayurvedic education. Thoughtful responses to these types of queries offer insight to make the best choice for your optimal well being. Certain traits and qualifications signify an Ayurvedic doctor's competence in Panchakarma therapies. Advanced specialty certification beyond general Ayurvedic education immerses practitioners wholly in the intensive modalities. Extensive hands-on experience administering hundreds of treatments under seasoned supervision hones skills. A holistic perspective understands preparatory and restorative protocols support the main therapies for thorough cleansing. Strong, compassionate communication enables custom-tailored recommendations based on close assessment rather than a one-size-fits-all approach. Membership in esteemed professional organizations suggests commitment to excellence and ongoing mastery through accountability. Individualization comes from recommending treatments aligned to each person's constitution, imbalance and circumstances. With proper training and experience comes the ability to safely manage cleansing reactions, making the process comfortable. And ultimately, look for selfless passion to serve others' well being rather than egoistic motives - this spirit touches the heart.

Reflecting on key questions also helps determine your optimal match. Do you feel genuinely heard, understood and respected? Do their qualifications and setting align with your needs? Are treatments personalized based on close examination versus generalized? Does the doctor patiently answer all concerns? Is Panchakarma their primary focus and do they have experience successfully treating clients with conditions like yours? What does your intuition say about how this practitioner fits your path? Only undertake this intensive therapy with someone you can trust, whose skillful care will support the depth of transformation possible when body, mind and soul are honored through the process.

To optimize the experience, communicate health history, goals and concerns transparently so protocols meet your needs. Prepare mentally, physically and emotionally by reading pre-cleanse guidelines. Arrange proper home support while away focusing wholly on healing. Bring creative tools to process experiences through journaling or art. Avoid over-scheduling post-cleanse to allow integration time. Set intentions to manifest positive changes. Let go of control and open to the process through patience and trust. Notice subtle healing shifts as well as dramatic ones. Track progress in a journal. Express any challenges so your provider can skillfully support you. Integrate recommended lifestyle practices afterwards. Appreciate the sacred inner growth and awakening that deep cleansing facilitates. Those who invest proper care into this profound therapy journey will reap rewarding outcomes.

5.6 Aftercare and Lifestyle Adjustments

Proper aftercare and lifestyle adjustments after Panchakarma allow the body to integrate deep cellular changes facilitated through cleansing. During initial post-cleanse days, focus on providing rest while eating light, easy-to-digest warm foods several times per day to gently rekindle digestive fire. Favor sweet, sour and salty tastes that strengthen the body rather than raw, cold or excess dry foods that weaken sensitive digestion. As strength returns over weeks, gradually reintroduce heavier foods like animal proteins, grains and dairy under practitioner guidance, noting any new sensitivities that arise. Prevent fatigue by not overexerting physically or mentally too quickly. Make time for meditation, breathwork, self-massage and reflection daily to release accumulated stress. Set intentions for positive changes aligned with long-term health goals.

Most importantly, appreciate and honor the profound inner shifts created through purification. Renewed energy can now focus on implementing uplifting habits and practices personalized to your unique mind-body constitution, rather than falling back into old unhealthy patterns. Continue choosing balancing foods, activities and lifestyle routines aligned with your cleansing insights.

A Comprehensive Journey into Ayurvedic Healing

As normal diet resumes, emphasize freshly cooked warm, unctuous and easy to digest meals while minimizing raw, cold or heavy foods that burden sensitive digestion post-cleanse. Reintroduce proteins, dairy, nuts and heavier grains incrementally over weeks as agni ignites. Reduce cold, raw, gas-producing foods still too dampening for rekindling fire. Stay hydrated with electrolyte water and herbal teas. Avoid overeating by reducing portions and stopping before fullness to prevent overwhelming weak digestion. Pay close attention to reactions as foods are added back to discern individual sensitivities. With gradual acclimation, agni will strengthen beyond its pre-cleanse state.

Likewise, integrate supportive lifestyle adjustments through this integration phase rather than immediately reinstating busy regimens. Get extra rest while minimizing obligations. Spend time alone in nature daily to realign with its healing rhythms. Journal thoughts, process emotions through creative outlets. Receive bodywork like massage and energy healing. Wait 1-3 months before new major responsibilities. Avoid chemical and electromagnetic toxins. Talk with spiritual counselors to integrate breakthroughs. Making self-care and introspection priorities allows Panchakarma's benefits to unfold and take root within your life.The weeks after Panchakarma establish patterns for maintaining balance long-term. Attune to nature's rhythms by aligning food choices, activities and self-care with the seasons to flow with external energies and maintain internal stability. Apply warming sesame or calming coconut oil before bathing to lubricate, pacify vata and release toxins. Periodically eliminate grains, dairy or certain foods for several days to rest the digestive tract. Once monthly, drink only water, juices or broths for 24 hours to give organs rest. Take triphala, dandelion and other cleansing herbs weekly to gently detoxify. Keep your digestive fire strong by eating at regular times, not overeating, avoiding cold drinks with meals and refraining from heavy foods when weak. Prioritize adequate deep sleep to rebuild tissues, clear wastes and establish healthy circadian rhythms. Boost ojas through yoga, meditation, creative arts, laughter, nature, relationships and reflection on higher truths. Obtain professional Panchakarma cleansing annually if possible to maintain balance. Consistency sustains optimal functioning unlocked through purification.

Signs of successful integration include feeling energized, mentally clear and emotionally stable with improved digestion and reduced chronic symptoms. Notice glowing skin, bright eyes, enhanced immunity, fitness and sleep as tissues renew. Appreciate heightened intuition, insight, purpose, peace, joy and spiritual connection. Feel motivated to care for your body, embrace simplicity and flow with life's changes. Desire pure diet, thoughts and environment. Positive adjustments indicate integration supported by wise choices sustaining rewarding gains.

Keys to anchoring these positive changes include remaining aware of subtle shifts, continuing practitioner support, gradual re-openings and simplification to avoid overwhelm. Process experiences creatively through art, music, writing. Talk with spiritual counselors to integrate emotional and spiritual openings. Commit to a daily self-care routine nourishing your unique needs. When cravings surface, pause and make conscious choices aligned with your goals. Keep healing intentions and self-knowledge front and center as motivation. Feel empowered by community support. Approach subsequent cleansing journeys with openness to deepen awakening. Honoring Panchakarma's gifts through nurturing integration allows profound benefits to permeate your life, anchoring positive evolution in body, mind and spirit.

Chapter 6

Herbal Remedies and Ayurvedic Pharmacology

6.1 Foundations of Ayurvedic Herbalism

Herbal remedies form a core part of Ayurvedic healing traditions. Drawing from a vast materia medica of plants, herbs, trees, minerals, metals, and animal products, Ayurvedic doctors can customize herbal formulas to suit each individual's constitution and imbalances. With origins dating back thousands of years, Ayurvedic herbalism is one of the world's oldest systems of natural medicine. Its remedies have stood the test of time for their safety, efficacy, and versatility in treating a wide range of health conditions.

In this chapter, we will explore the foundations and key principles of Ayurvedic herbalism. You will learn about some of the most important Ayurvedic herbs and their medicinal properties. We discuss how Ayurvedic herbal formulas are prepared based on combinations of herbs to achieve targeted results. You will also gain an understanding of proper dosage, quality control, and sustainable sourcing of Ayurvedic herbs in today's globalized world. Finally, you will discover some simple, commonly used Ayurvedic herbal remedies that you can begin using at home to support the health and balance of body, mind, and consciousness.

The origins of Ayurveda's vast materia medica can be traced back to the Vedas, India's oldest spiritual scriptures which date back as far as 6,000 to 8,000 BCE. The Atharva Veda in particular contains detailed information about the identification and uses of medicinal plants, describing properties of herbs growing in the foothills of the Himalayas to tropical zones. Early Ayurvedic texts such as the Charaka Samhita (circa 700 BCE) and Sushruta Samhita (circa 600 BCE) expanded on the Vedas' foundation, elaborating on the characteristics and therapeutic indications of hundreds more medicinal plants and minerals.

From ancient times until today, knowledge of Ayurvedic herbalism has been passed down from teacher to student through both spiritual texts and direct clinical training. Contemporary Ayurvedic doctors still rely primarily on classic texts like the Charaka Samhita as source material to guide their use of herbs. However, they also incorporate modern pharmacological research and clinical observations into their repertoire. Some of the most commonly used Ayurvedic herbs have now been studied extensively for their phytochemical makeup and mechanisms of action on human physiology. Combining this scientific knowledge with Ayurveda's thousand-year-old holistic healing framework allows practitioners to unleash the full power of herbs to heal and transform the body.

Ayurveda classifies medicinal substances primarily by six tastes (rasas) and twenty qualities (gunas). Each herb has a unique combination of these tastes and qualities which determines how it will interact with the human body and mind. For example, pungent, bitter herbs tend to stimulate digestion and clear stagnation, while sweet, salty herbs nourish, strengthen, and calm. Beyond basic qualities, Ayurveda also classifies herbs based on their targeted effects on specific body tissues (dhatus) and metabolic pathways (srotas). An intricate understanding of these classifications allows Ayurvedic doctors to create customized herbal formulas for individual patients.

Single herbs rarely act in isolation, however. Ayurveda employs synergistic combinations of multiple herbs in most formulations to enhance effectiveness and allow for smaller, safer doses. Formulas may contain 5-50 herbs carefully selected and proportioned to complement each other. Some herbs direct the formula toward certain body tissues or organs needing healing. Other herbs support absorption and delivery of active compounds to target areas. Still others provide a harmonizing effect to balance potential side effects of the primary herbs. Skillfully combining herbs in this way is what gives Ayurvedic remedies their power and versatility.

Humanity has only scratched the surface of the myriad healing plants used in the Ayurvedic materia medica. However, some herbs stand out as being both widely available and frequently used by Ayurvedic practitioners across India and beyond. Here, we introduce a selection of these ""superherbs"" that form the backbone of the Ayurvedic apothecary:

Turmeric (Curcuma longa): The golden spice turmeric needs little introduction for its bright yellow color and prevalence in curry dishes. Used for thousands of years in Ayurveda and other Asian medical systems, turmeric is one of the most extensively researched medicinal plants. The curcumin compound gives turmeric its vibrant color and therapeutic properties: antioxidant, anti-inflammatory, antiseptic, analgesic, and immunomodulatory. Turmeric treats digestive and liver disorders, arthritis and joint pain, diabetes, high cholesterol, autoimmunity, headaches, and more. It can be taken as a powder, tablet, tea, milk decoction, or applied topically for first aid.

Ashwagandha (Withania somnifera): A premier rejuvenating herb in Ayurveda, ashwagandha builds vitality, sexual potency, muscle strength, and stamina while also calming the nervous system. It treats insomnia, fatigue, low immunity, anxiety, poor cognition, and weakness from old age or illness. Ashwagandha stabilizes mood and hormone levels through its adaptogenic action which balances the entire body. The root powder can be mixed into warm milk or water at night.

A Comprehensive Journey into Ayurvedic Healing

Neem (Azadirachta indica): Neem is a tropical evergreen tree native to India revered for its antifungal, antibacterial, and antiviral properties. Every part of the neem tree has medicinal value, from the bark and leaves to seeds and oil. Neem cleanses the blood, supports the liver and immune system, heals skin diseases and ulcers, and protects connective tissues. It makes an effective preventative health tonic against infection when taken regularly as tea, tablets, or leaf powder.

Amalaki (Phyllanthus emblica): Also known as Indian gooseberry, amalaki fruit is one of the richest natural sources of vitamin C and antioxidants. In Ayurveda, amalaki cools excess Pitta in the digestive tract, blood, and liver, relieving acidity, ulcers, dysentery, anemia, and jaundice. It nourishes the body's tissues and boosts immunity against infection. Amalaki treats premature aging and greying of hair when taken regularly. It combines synergistically with turmeric in the traditional formula Triphala.

Ginger (Zingiber officinale): A universal home remedy across cultures, ginger is indispensable in Ayurvedic herbalism for itsDigestion-enhancing and detoxifying powers. It alleviates nausea, bloating, indigestion, and heaviness after eating. Ginger improves circulation, warms the extremities, and dissolves clumped Kapha/ama in the channels. Chewing raw ginger stimulates digestion before a meal. Boiled and steeped into a tea, it relieves gas and abdominal pain when sipped after eating. Ginger also enhances the bioavailability of other herbs taken along with it.While Ayurvedic doctors today have an array of modern formulations and delivery methods available, traditional methods for preparing medicines remain popular and relevant. The most common classical dosage forms include churnas which are powdered mixes of herbs and minerals that can be blended into honey, ghee, water, or cooked foods for gentle absorption. Churnas treat a wide variety of imbalances from high cholesterol to nervous disorders with Triphala, the three-fruit blend, being a famous example. There are also asavas and arishtas which are fermented preparations made by steeping herbs in water and sugar cane juice for several weeks or months. The fermentation process increases potency and absorption of asavas, which improve digestion and metabolization, and arishtas, which are restorative tonics for depleted states. Guggulus are extracts of guggulu resin combined with herbs to enhance penetration into tissues and effectively reduce inflammation, arthritis, and high cholesterol. The guggulu plant has anti-inflammatory action similar to ibuprofen. Bhasmas are herbo-mineral formulas reduced through calcination into ultrafine nanoparticle powders that strengthen bones and nerves, imparting ojas-essence. Proper preparation neutralizes toxic heavy metals in the source material of bhasmas.

With the rising popularity of Ayurvedic herbs worldwide, proper regulation, quality control, and responsible prescribing are essential to protect consumers. Certain Ayurvedic herbs contain toxic heavy metals like mercury, arsenic, lead, and cadmium that should only be used internally in potent bhasma forms meeting modern safety standards. For commercial herbal products, quality control testing for heavy metals and microbial contaminants is critical, with regulations being stricter in some countries than others. Buying reputable brands from sustainable sources helps minimize risks. Ayurvedic herbal supplements often use concentrated powdered extracts for higher potency and easier dosing which increases the potential for interactions and overdose when self-prescribed incorrectly. Practitioners determine optimal dosage by considering the patient's age, size, sensitivity, and health issues. Following the dosage guidelines on supplement labels carefully and starting conservatively with lower doses when trying new remedies is wise. Certain herbs taken in excess can have serious side effects or negatively impact pre-existing conditions. Telling your doctor about any Ayurvedic supplements you take allows monitoring for interactions with prescription medications.

With some guidance on safety and sourcing, you can begin using simple Ayurvedic remedies to support health and balance daily. Adding 1/2 teaspoon turmeric and ginger powders and a dash of black pepper into

A Comprehensive Journey into Ayurvedic Healing

warm milk makes a classic Ayurvedic tonic to boost digestion and immunity at night. Brewing a calming tea with equal parts ashwagandha, licorice root, fennel, and cinnamon and taking it after dinner provides anxiety relief and restful sleep. For indigestion, heartburn, or gas, stirring 1/2 teaspoon Triphala powder into a glass of warm water and drinking 30 minutes after eating can help. Massaging warmed Brahmi oil infused with Gotu Kola onto the scalp before bed nourishes hair follicles and calms the mind. Rubbing a salve containing Dashmool herbs and ginger onto affected areas can increase circulation and mobility for joint pain and stiffness. Taking a 500mg Trikatu capsule with meals during allergy season or illness clears sinus congestion as the heating combo of ginger, black pepper and pippali. Mixing a pinch of ground Triphala in a small amount of honey and applying it to the teeth and gums twice daily reduces bacteria and inflammation.

The global demand for Ayurvedic herbs has given rise to large-scale commercialized harvesting from wild plant populations. Unethical over-harvesting threatens the diversity and survival of ancient medicinal plants in their native habitats, with certain coveted species like sandalwood even facing extinction in the wild. Ayurvedic doctors and consumers must prioritize sustainability when using herbs by supporting suppliers practicing responsible organic farming, wild harvesting techniques and fair trade business models to ensure an abundant future supply. Buying from companies donating proceeds to ecological conservation provides additional impact. Seeking out Ayurvedic herbs grown domestically can reduce the energy footprint of overseas shipping. Whenever possible, growing your own herbs at home, even just a few potted basil, turmeric and aloe plants, makes a meaningful difference. With mindful stewardship, the precious medicinal plants that sustain Ayurvedic healing traditions can thrive for generations to come.

In summary, Ayurveda's vast materia medica offers natural healing remedies for nearly any imbalance one may face. Equipped with foundational knowledge of major Ayurvedic herbs, you can safely begin incorporating herbal supplements and home preparations into your health regimen for deep, lasting wellbeing while honoring the ancient origins of Ayurvedic plant wisdom through ethical sourcing and sustainable use."

6.2 Major Ayurvedic Herbs and Their Uses

The use of herbs and plant-based ingredients has been an integral part of Ayurvedic medicine and healing for thousands of years. Ayurveda's herbal tradition developed significantly during the time when medical schools known as gurukulas flourished in ancient India. Students at these schools carefully studied the therapeutic properties of flowers, leaves, roots, bark and seeds under the close guidance of learned Ayurvedic masters. Extensive manuscripts detailing countless natural remedies were compiled to be passed down through the generations. Today, this valuable herb knowledge continues to be used by Ayurvedic practitioners all over the world.

Some of the most essential herbs in Ayurvedic pharmacology include time-honored staples that have been relied upon since ancient times. Their Sanskrit names may be unfamiliar to Western ears, yet many have now become better known globally. These key Ayurvedic herbs offer gentle healing and prevention for a wide variety of common health issues. Getting to know them provides insight into how natural substances can foster wellbeing with minimal side effects when used properly.

Triphala is arguably the most revered Ayurvedic herbal formula. Consisting of three dried fruits—amalaki, bibhitaki and haritaki—it possesses a uniquely balancing and rejuvenating influence. Known as a rasayana or rejuvenative in Ayurveda, triphala gently maintains regular bowel function, aids digestion and absorption, reduces occasional gas and bloating, and promotes healthy cholesterol and blood sugar levels. It's no wonder this formula has remained popular for centuries! The three triphala fruits offer a mild laxative effect when needed, yet they also bolster the entire digestive system in a holistic way. For maintaining gastrointestinal wellness, eliminating wastes, and preventing disease, triphala is still unsurpassed today. Recommended dosage is around 500mg taken before bed or upon rising with warm water.

Turmeric draws its vivid golden-orange color from beneficial antioxidant compounds called curcuminoids. The most studied curcuminoid is curcumin, which has been extensively researched for its anti-inflammatory and antioxidant capabilities. Turmeric has long been valued in Ayurveda for supporting joint health, vitality, circulation, immunity and emotional balance. It is also revered for its ability to stimulate digestion despite having heating energetics. The typical dosage for supplemental turmeric extract is 400mg to 600mg per day but amounts up to 3000mg may be used therapeutically. Cooking with the whole turmeric root in curries and vegetable dishes allows absorption of valuable oils as well. Those with bile duct blockages should avoid turmeric.

Ginger is another popular Ayurvedic staple known as a warming herb that aids digestion and absorption in the gastrointestinal tract. Its gnarled roots contain bioactive compounds like gingerols and shogaols that provide relief for nausea, diarrhea, cramping and other digestive woes. Ginger also has a penetrating effect that helps guide other herbs to where they are needed most in the body. Dried ginger powder can be taken in 250mg to 500mg amounts up to three times daily for therapeutic purposes. For nausea, ginger tea or ginger slices simmered in water work well. Limit ginger during pregnancy unless advised by a physician. People with ulcers or acid reflux should also use caution with it.

Ashwagandha has emerged as one of the most sought after Ayurvedic herbs today due to extensive scientific research on its stress-relieving and energy-boosting powers. Also called Indian ginseng or winter cherry, ashwagandha helps counteract many negative effects of chronic stress when taken regularly. Adaptogenic herbs like ashwagandha strengthen resistance to all types of physical, mental and emotional stressors. Ashwagandha encourages restful sleep, mental calmness, enhanced focus and thyroid health. Typical doses range from 300mg to 600mg daily of standardized extract, though some people may benefit from doses up to 2000mg short term. Ashwagandha is very safe but should be avoided in pregnancy.

Manjistha is an incredible Ayurvedic herb for keeping blood clean and skin glowing. It purifies the blood by removing toxins and bolstering lymph drainage and has traditionally been used to clear skin congestion and discoloration. Manjistha supplements help minimize acne breakouts while improving the quality and texture of the skin. It also enhances circulation and may reduce enlarged lymph nodes. Doses around 500mg once or twice daily are considered effective and safe. Manjistha works well when combined with other blood and lymph cleansing herbs like dandelion, burdock and red clover. Those already on blood thinning medication should exercise caution with it.

Neem is known for having bitter, cooling and antibacterial qualities that discourage harmful organisms internally and topically on the skin. All parts of the neem tree have therapeutic effects — leaves, flowers, bark, seeds and seed oil. For skin health, neem oil makes an excellent addition to creams, salves and soaps. Internally, neem supplements can minimize yeast overgrowth and support immune response in the GI tract. Neem is very safe and gentle but higher doses may not be suitable during pregnancy. Capsules with 500mg to 1,000mg taken twice per day help purify the body on a deeper level. Neem toothpastes and mouth rinses also freshen breath and protect gums.

A Comprehensive Journey into Ayurvedic Healing

Shatavari is perhaps the most beloved Ayurvedic herb for women's health. Translated as "she who possesses 100 husbands" in Sanskrit, it refers to the herb's ability to provide vitality and soothing moisture to the female reproductive system. Shatavari balances hormones and helps regulate menses. For menstrual cramps, PMS, perimenopause, low libido and fertility enhancement, shatavari has been relied upon for centuries. Doses around 500mg twice daily are traditionally used but amounts up to 2000mg may be advised by Ayurvedic practitioners. Shatavari combines exceptionally well with ashwagandha, licorice and vidari kanda. Avoid shatavari with estrogen-sensitive cancers.

Boswellia serrata is the Ayurvedic herb that produces an aromatic resin called frankincense. This ancient plant medicine has been prized since antiquity for its ability to support healthy inflammatory response and joint comfort. Modern research confirms boswellia's traditional uses for arthritis, injury trauma and other pain-producing conditions. Boswellia extracts inhibit pro-inflammatory compounds in the body, allowing it to provide fast-acting yet sustained relief. Doses start around 300mg daily but some take up to 1800mg for therapeutic effects. Boswellia is very well tolerated and can be used for extended periods safely unless allergic to it.While single herbs offer tremendous healing benefits, Ayurveda also emphasizes synergistic herbal formulations for enhancing potency. Certain herbs work better in combination by capitalizing on each other's therapeutic actions. Ayurvedic texts describe many classic preparations pairing herbs together, though formulations are often tailored to individual needs as well. Some Ayurvedic products feature nearly a dozen herbs or more crafted into precisely calibrated formulas. Though this may seem complicated, the holistic combinations only serve to improve efficacy and versatility.

Chyawanprash is one of the most beloved Ayurvedic combinations. This nutritional jam contains Indian gooseberry plus dozens of herbs cooked and blended together with honey, sesame oil, ghee and cane sugar. It was first created for the sage Chyawan to restore his vitality and exemplifies a rejuvenative rasayana formula. Just a teaspoon daily provides antioxidants, micronutrients and adaptogens that bolster immunity, digestion, respiratory health and more. Chyawanprash makes an excellent tonic for children and the elderly too. It can be enjoyed straight off the spoon or stirred into milk or warm water. Those with diabetes should limit sugar intake from this supplement.

The Ayurvedic detox formula Triphala Guggulu skillfully merges triphala's digestive and eliminative effects with the cleansing actions of guggulu, also known as guggul or Indian myrrh. Guggulu resin has been used in Ayurveda for centuries to scrape away stubborn wastes and rejuvenate tissues. It also enhances circulation and supports joint comfort. Combining triphala with guggulu creates a powerful aid for weight management, lipid balance, gentle detoxification, and maintaining an already healthy inflammation response. The typical dosage is 500mg to 1000mg once or twice daily. Those on blood thinners or with upcoming surgery should avoid guggulu.

Stress-relieving Ayurvedic formulations like Ashwagandha Brahm Rasayan and Mind-RP leverage the strength of prime herbs ashwagandha, brahmi, shankhpushpi and jatamansi. These central nervous system tonics calm overactivity, nourish mental functioning, improve concentration and allow relaxation. A personalized combination of several adaptogens and nervines can resolve mind-body exhaustion, disturbed sleep, racing thoughts and burnout. Start with lower doses around 300mg once or twice daily and increase cautiously if needed. While these formulations are extremely safe, those taking psychiatric medications should proceed with care.

The Ayurvedic compound Sitopaladi Churna demonstrates the synergistic power of combining parts of several plants together. In this case, sugar cane, cardamom, cinnamon, licorice root and other warming spices join forces to bolster respiratory health. Sitopaladi is revered as a rasayana for the lungs that liquefies mucus while building immunity against pathogens. It provides gentle antioxidant, anti-inflammatory and mucolytic support that opens airways. This is an excellent remedy for chronic sinus congestion, coughs, sore throat and seasonal allergies. Doses around 500mg to 1000mg can be taken up to three times per day as needed. Those with high blood pressure should moderate licorice intake.

Pharmacological principles are found throughout classical Ayurvedic texts advising how to combine herbs intentionally based on energetics, ratios, delivery vehicles and compatibility. Some formulations bring together herbs of similar qualities, while others artfully blend opposing forces to achieve balance. Certain master herbs known as yogavahi transport the potency deep into bodily tissues. Still other Ayurvedic preparations rely on alchemy, gems or ritualized consecration to further enhance benefits. Though ancient in origin, Ayurveda's sophisticated herbal technology still provides inspiration for modern naturopathic remedies that gently heal.

When it comes to consuming Ayurvedic herbal supplements regularly or giving them to children, quality and safety are paramount. Reputable Ayurvedic companies test raw herbs and finished products thoroughly for bacterial contamination and heavy metals. Organic, sustainably wildcrafted or fair trade herbs harvested at optimal potency should be used. Banyan Botanicals, Maharishi Ayurveda, Organic India and other brands follow stringent quality protocols. Consulting an Ayurvedic practitioner helps determine which herbs and dosages are right for your unique needs and sensitivities. Standardized modern manufacturing procedures ensure purity, potency and effectiveness meeting FDA guidelines.

Some Ayurvedic herbal supplements are now readily available over-the-counter for home use. Chyawanprash, triphala tablets, guggulu and digestive formulas like Hingashtak Churna make digestive regularity easier. Ashwagandha, brahmi, gotu kola and shatavari support calmness, cognitive functioning and female reproductive health. Respiratory formulas like sitopaladi or kantakari lubricate the lungs and sinuses. Topical oil blends soothe muscles and joints while neem cream clears problem skin. With professional guidance, these gentle yet powerful herbals foster wellbeing, resilience and inner harmony.

Ultimately, reverence for nature itself forms the foundation of Ayurveda's herbal wisdom. Ayurveda teaches that plants are conscious beings that sacrifice themselves for humanity's welfare when harvested ethically. We must honor these green healers with grateful and compassionate hearts. Sustainable harvesting ensures their continued availability while minimizing environmental impact. By honoring plant spirits that bestow their medicinal gifts, Ayurveda's herbal legacy endures as a living testament to humanity's intimate connection with nature. Our health and wholeness relies upon skillfully utilizing plant blessings while caring for the Earth that sustains us all."

6.3 Preparing Ayurvedic Formulas and Medicines

While Ayurveda's approach to herbalism may seem simple on the surface, the process of crafting traditional formulas and medicines follows a refined art and science. Practical yet visionary, Ayurvedic pharmacology combines herbal wisdom, medical knowledge and even spiritual insight into creating remedies that restore wholeness on every level. Though modern methods now ensure quality and consistency, Ayurveda's holistic mindset continues to distinguish its remedies from conventional medicine.

The foundational Ayurvedic texts known as Samhitas describe numerous methods and materials for preparing herbal formulations. Cold infusion, hot infusion, fermentation, decoction and calcination each extract specific properties from herbs using water, oil, sugar, alcohol or heat. Additional ingredients like pungent spices, minerals or

A Comprehensive Journey into Ayurvedic Healing

animal products augment the benefits in precise ways. The finished medicines encompass medicated ghees, fermented wines, essential oil blends, herbal jams, powdered formulas and pill products.

Vaidyas, or Ayurvedic physicians, carefully customize combinations by considering the patient's constitution, imbalance, digestive strength, age and stage of illness. The synergy and compatibility among constituent herbs determines optimal ratios. Delivery vehicles influence how quickly effects manifest and where they concentrate in the body. For example, ghee penetrates rapidly while medicated oils seep deeply into tissues. The complexity reaches an art form requiring wisdom and experience to master. Yet the goal of bringing about authentic healing remains pure.

The caliber of ingredients and meticulousness of preparation significantly impacts an Ayurvedic formula's healing potential. Use of fresh, organic or wildcrafted herbs picked at peak potency ensures higher levels of active compounds. Cleanliness, precision and mindfulness elevate the remedies energetically. Mantras chanted during cooking infuse vibrational healing. Treating ingredients as living beings magnifies their consciousness. Proper preparatory steps not only extract chemical constituents but retain subtle energy. Although shortcuts exist today, preserving these subtleties distinguishes Ayurveda's legacy.

Government regulations, laboratory testing and good manufacturing practices now provide additional quality control, safety and standardization for Ayurvedic products. Reputable companies thoroughly analyze raw materials and finished goods. Conservationist sourcing, eco-friendly extraction and fair trade practices generate sustainable, high quality herbal supplements. However, the human hand, heart and intuition remain instrumental in manifesting Ayurveda's herbal wisdom. With holistic understanding and right effort, potent plant medicines emerge.

The common kitchen spice turmeric provides an accessible example of preparing and using Ayurvedic herbs at home. Turmeric roots can be dried and pulverized into powder for cooking. The powder infused into warm milk makes a nourishing nighttime tonic. Turmeric, ginger and black pepper boiled into a tea supports digestion. For topical relief, turmeric powder simmered into oil or ghee extracts soothing, antioxidant compounds. Taking these simple steps with awareness harnesses turmeric's full benefits.

Triphala is also very easy to use for home health. The dried fruits simply need powdering before taking as a digestive supplement. For removing toxins, triphala powder is steeped overnight in water. A traditional Ayurvedic practice involves consuming this liquid on an empty stomach first thing in the morning. Triphala ghee and oils can be prepared by heating the powder gently into these lipid bases. Practicing these basic Ayurvedic preparations maximizes triphala's potency in a convenient form.

Ashwagandha, Brahmi and other Ayurvedic herbs also lend themselves well to at-home remedies. Ashwagandha and warm milk enhance sleep and recovery. Brahmi-infused oil calms the mind when massaged into the scalp. Even just taking Chyawanprash, Dashamoola or Trikatu tablets provides daily herbal nutrition. Simple yet profound, home preparations sustain awareness of food as medicine. With basic kitchen tools and quality herbs, we partake in Ayurveda's herbal wisdom that nourishes body, mind and soul.

Developing a relationship with Ayurvedic plants brings their benefits directly into your life. Growing culinary herbs like basil, cilantro, fennel and mint yields fresh ingredients for cooking therapeutic meals. The garden's tranquility fosters meditation. Herbs grown with natural sunlight and care exude vitality. Ayurveda views plants as manifestations of divine consciousness honoring the interdependence between people and nature. Connecting with herbs spiritually awakens their healing potential and your own.When taking Ayurvedic herbal supplements regularly or giving them to children, proper dosing ensures effectiveness and safety. Traditional Ayurvedic forms like ghee, oils, jams and wines make dosing trickier than capsules or tablets. Practitioners advise conservative amounts initially with gradual increases as needed. Typical doses for dried herbs are 500mg to 1,000mg per day but may range up to 5,000mg in some protocols. Concentrated extracts have different dosage guidelines. Children require smaller amounts customized by weight and age.

Always follow the dosage instructions on supplement labels or provided by your Ayurvedic specialist. Certain herbs taken in excess or by sensitive persons can cause side effects. For example, too much liquorice may elevate blood pressure. Iron-rich herbs like ashwagandha could aggravate hemochromatosis. A qualified Ayurvedic practitioner considers your case intricacies when advising dosages. Their guidance optimizes benefits while minimizing risks. Practicing moderation, listening to your body and seeking expert consultation keeps Ayurvedic herbal use safe.

Potential drug interactions must also be weighed when combining Ayurvedic supplements with conventional medications. Herbs like guggulu, garlic and ginseng have anti-clotting effects that can be problematic with blood thinners like Coumadin. Immune-boosting herbs may interact with immunosuppressant drugs. Sedating nervines like brahmi and jatamansi could compound anesthesia. Since possible interactions exist, inform your healthcare providers about Ayurvedic remedies you take and seek medical guidance. With vigilance, herbal supplements and pharmaceuticals can often be taken together constructively.

Allergic reactions to Ayurvedic herbs are uncommon but can occur with any botanical. Stop taking any formula that causes rashes, hives, swelling or breathing problems. Consult an Ayurvedic physician to determine suitable alternatives since allergies are often dose-dependent. High quality Ayurvedic supplements made under GMP rarely have contaminants, yet subpar products could pose toxicity risks if improperly manufactured. Purchase reputable brands through trusted suppliers and be wary of overly cheap products. With prudence, herbalism's sensitive wisdom brings wholeness.

Ethical and ecologically sustainable practices now ensure Ayurveda's herbal legacy continues benefiting humanity for generations to come. Select suppliers that honor fair trade principles and cultivate healing plants organically at peak potency. Seek herbs wild-harvested respectfully from clean natural habitats without endangering native species. Choosing reforested, renewable herbs like guduchi, amalaki and ashwagandha protects nature's gifts. Ayurveda's true spirit values environmental preservation alongside human health. Through conscientious stewardship today, the ancient wisdom of herbal healing lives on.

As humanity rediscovers traditional plant medicines, we carry forward Ayurveda's herbal sophistication in modern forms. Blending holistic wellness insights with quality control, scientific study and commercial availability revives this knowledge for modern times. Yet we must honor the sacred spirit in nature that offers her healing riches to those who respect her. By adopting Ayurveda's universal vision that interconnectedness underlies all life, we appreciate how returning traditional herbal wisdom to people and the planet brings awakening for humanity and our Earth home.

6.4 Safety, Quality, and Dosages

The healing power of Ayurvedic herbs relies on skillful preparation, responsible dosing and choosing reputable products. Remedial plants offer profound benefits when used with wisdom and care. While Ayurveda's herbal legacy remained pure for centuries, modern quality control now ensures these age-old remedies meet safety and potency standards. A few key considerations help optimize the effectiveness of Ayurvedic herbal supplements in contemporary times.

Selecting products made by companies following Good Manufacturing Practices (GMP) provides assurance of quality. Rigorous quality testing should analyze raw herbs for identification, heavy metals, microbes and pesticides. Batch-to-batch consistency relies on precision from farm to finished goods. GMP facilities validate manufacturing processes, equipment and training. While more costly, compliance protects consumers. Reputable brands like Banyan Botanicals and Organic India validate premium quality standards.

The dosage makes the medicine as the saying goes, so following label instructions for Ayurvedic herbs is important. Traditional Ayurvedic formulas may seem low-dosed but act synergistically in the body. Some modern extractions or concentrates use higher amounts. Consult an Ayurvedic practitioner to determine optimal dosing for your needs and sensitivities. They'll consider your constitution, age, digestive strength and medical conditions. Never take more than recommended without guidance. Careful dosing maximizes benefits and satisfaction.

Seeking organic and ethically wild-harvested herbs also enhances therapeutic value. Plants grown naturally and harvested sustainably retain vitality and potency better. Organic farming avoids toxic pesticides and chemical residues that are concentrated in herbs. Sustainable wild collection prevents habitat destruction and over-foraging of rare species. Fair trade principles help local communities benefit equitably from botanical commerce. When possible, choose Ayurvedic herbs cultivated regeneratively, although premium quality costs more.

Storing Ayurvedic supplements properly preserves potency. Keep products in cool, dry places away from direct light, moisture and heat. Refrigeration prolongs freshness for oils, ghees and certain formulas as indicated. Shelflife varies from months to years if unopened—check expiry dates and observe changes. Reorder three months before products expire for continuity. Proper home storage makes Ayurvedic herbs more economical and effective. Discard any rancid, degrading or contaminated products you wouldn't consume.

Many Ayurvedic herbs grown in India test higher in heavy metals due to industrial pollution. Reputable companies like Banyan Botanicals, Organic India and Maharishi Ayurveda reject contaminated ingredients during thorough testing. If concerned, choose supplements made with herbs cultivated in cleaner growing regions or domestically. Certain herbs like shilajit and bhasmas contain trace minerals naturally but should still meet quality limits. Voicing preferences for purity encourages production improvements worldwide.

Potential sensitivities must also be considered when using Ayurvedic herbs regularly. While most people tolerate them well, reactions can occasionally occur. Allergies are rare but stop taking any formula causing hives, rashes or swelling. Also discontinue herbs upsetting digestion, sleep or mood. Seek professional guidance to find suitable alternatives since reactions often relate to dosage. With close observation, herbals bring wellness gently.

Ayurvedic herbalism honors the natural intelligence inherent in plants to restore wholeness. Developing a personal relationship with botanical allies awakens their healing potential. Observe changes after starting supplements with impartiality. Check for improved digestion, elimination, energy, immunity, sleep, moods and inner calm. Keeping an herbal journal aids monitoring. Through experiential learning, we comprehend Ayurveda's herbal wisdom. Greater vitality, clarity and inner silence become the best indicators of effectiveness.

While Ayurveda's herbal treasures offer powerful healing, how we relate to plants also impacts wellbeing. Relating to botanicals respectfully as conscious beings who sacrificially offer medicinal gifts fosters reciprocal connection. Gratitude and compassion for their generosity reminds us of humanity's interdependence with the natural world. Ayurveda's holistic paradigm honors beneficial plants as manifestations of nature's infinite intelligence and grace.Ayurveda's time-honored herbal wisdom offers natural healing with minimal risks when used properly. Still, certain precautions help ensure safety and satisfaction when taking supplements regularly. Avoid herbs during pregnancy and breastfeeding unless specifically advised by your healthcare provider. Check for possible supplement interactions with medications you take to prevent problems. Introduce children to gentle Ayurvedic herbs like brahmi and amla but use conservative doses suitable for their age and size.

While most people can take Ayurvedic remedies without issues, occasional sensitivity reactions are possible. Discontinue any formula causing nausea, diarrhea, dizziness, rash or headache. Try lower doses of that herb again later or opt for a different alternative. Seeking guidance from an Ayurvedic specialist finds suitable options since constitution and dosing play roles. With attentive observation, herbal supplements bring wellness gently.

Certain health conditions warrant care when using Ayurvedic herbs. Those with diabetes should monitor blood sugar closely since some herbs impact glycemic control. People with clotting factor deficiencies or on blood thinners must avoid supplements that increase bleeding risks. Check with your doctor about kidney or liver conditions, upcoming surgery or immune dysfunction before taking unfamiliar herbs. Though gentle, Ayurveda's herbal wisdom deserves respect.

While Ayurvedic herbs offer therapeutic advantages, relying excessively on supplements overlooks the wholistic paradigm. Primarily adopt lifestyle measures like optimal diet, routines, detoxification and yoga first. Add herbs strategically to support natural balance when needed. They serve best as tonics that augment health, not pharmacological fixes taken perpetually. Purify imbalances with Panchakarma or fasting to minimize supplement dependence. Herbs work best holistically.

Sourcing high quality Ayurvedic products from reputable suppliers also enhances therapeutic success. With proliferating consumer demand comes increased incentives for profiteering through dubious means. Seek authentic formulas from companies honoring Ayurveda's essence. Beware of proprietary blends lacking transparency or overly complex products deviating from tradition. Simplicity and integrity differentiate true herbal wisdom. Let purity of purpose and practice be the guide.

Ultimately Ayurveda's herbal legacy demonstrates most powerfully through inner transformation of consciousness. While physical and mental health naturally improve, deeper benefits emerge. As we honor the sacred interconnection between humanity and nature, superficial identification with the body-mind releases. We touch our spiritual essence beyond time, space and karma. This realization of eternal Onenessaligned with the Universal Source brings freedom, unconditional inner peace and transcendent understanding. Ayurveda's herbal gifts offer vehicles for awakening.

By integrating Ayurveda's herbal wisdom into modern lifestyles conscientiously, we ready this ancient science of life to uplift humanity's future. Judicious quality controls ensure safety and effectiveness for generations to come. Sourcing herbs sustainably makes their benefits accessible and renewable. Adapting traditional preparations for easy use in suitable doses makes Ayurvedic herbalism practical today. Respecting the sanctity of plants fosters a spirituality of interdependence, compassion and Dharma. Honoring those who came before while advancing knowledge carries Ayurveda forward.

6.5 Common Remedies for Home Use

A Comprehensive Journey into Ayurvedic Healing

While potent Ayurvedic herbs and formulas offer therapeutic advantages, many gentle remedies make home use convenient, safe and effective. Taking certain supplements regularly fosters natural balance, energy and inner calm. Even beginners can easily integrate Ayurvedic herbs into daily routines for wellbeing support. Learning a few common staples provides a solid foundation for delving deeper into Ayurveda's herbal wisdom.

Triphala is arguably the most essential Ayurvedic formula to keep on hand for home health. Composed of the dried fruits of amalaki, haritaki and bibhitaki, triphala uniquely supports many aspects of wellness. Its mild laxative effect promotes healthy regularity and detoxification. Triphala also enhances digestion and assimilation of nutrients. It minimizes acidity, bloating and inflammation in the gastrointestinal tract. Rich in antioxidants, triphala boosts immunity and delays aging. For these myriad benefits, triphala remains unsurpassed as an everyday tonic.

Ashwagandha, also known as Indian ginseng, stands out among rejuvenative herbs known as adaptogens. Extensive research confirms its anti-stress and antioxidant properties. Ashwagandha relieves exhaustion by moderating cortisol levels. It enhances energy, endurance and concentration while reducing anxiety. Ashwagandha also promotes restful sleep, making it highly versatile. The optimal dosage ranges from 300-500mg daily of concentrated extract. Larger amounts up to 2000mg provide additional therapeutic effects. The only contraindication is avoiding ashwagandha during pregnancy.

Ginger root serves as an excellent warming digestive aid to keep on hand. Fresh ginger brewed into tea relieves nausea, cramping, bloating and diarrhea. Its bioactive compounds soothe gastrointestinal inflammation and stimulate digestion. For supplement use, doses around 500mg daily maximize benefits. Consuming raw ginger regularly also supports health, or cooking with it adds flavor and medicinal value to foods.

People with gallstones should avoid large amounts of ginger. Otherwise it is very safe and pairs well with many other herbs.

Turmeric root also offers versatile therapeutic advantages through its primary active compound curcumin. Prized for its anti-inflammatory, antioxidant and antibacterial properties, turmeric improves circulation, immunity and cellular health. Curcumin aids joint comfort, memory, liver function and mood balance. Cooking with turmeric or taking around 500mg daily harnesses these far-reaching benefits. Curcumin is poorly absorbed alone so combine with pepper and fat for greater bioavailability. Those with bile duct blockage should avoid turmeric.

Gotu kola is an Ayurvedic herb traditionally used to enhance memory, cognition and longevity. Sometimes called brahmi (not Bacopa monnieri), gotu kola counters anxiety, fatigue and hyperactivity in children. It provides antioxidant protection especially for nerves and brain cells. Gotu kola appears to increase intelligence and calmness when taken regularly. The typical dosage is around 500mg per day of the extract. No serious side effects are known except avoiding gotu kola during pregnancy.

Guggulu is the resin from the Indian myrrh tree that offers potent cleansing and rejuvenating actions. It effectively scrapes away stubborn accumulated wastes while lubricating joints and enhancing circulation. Guggulu also optimizes cholesterol levels already in normal range and dismantles cysts, benign growths and clots. For supplement use, a typical guggulu dosage is around 500mg daily. Those on blood thinners or with upcoming surgery should avoid guggulu because of its mild anticoagulant effects.

Brahmi (Bacopa monnieri) is perhaps the most legendary Ayurvedic mental tonic for enhancing learning, memory and awareness. Brahmi uniquely improves concentration, cognition and intelligence while reducing stress and anxiety. Traditionally brahmi oil was massaged into the scalp daily to nourish the nervous system. Now brahmi extracts provide similar benefits at oral doses around 500mg daily. No serious side effects are known except avoiding brahmi during pregnancy and for young children.

Amla, or Indian gooseberry, provides exceptional antioxidant protection that supports natural immunity and wellness. Rich in vitamin C and polyphenols, amla fights infection, balances stomach acidity, enhances Liver function, and reduces inflammation. Dried amla fruit chewed daily promotes oral health and assimilation of nutrients. For supplement use, 500mg to 1,000mg daily strengthens defenses against disease and aging. No adverse effects are expected at typical doses. Amla makes an excellent tonic for people of all ages.Several Ayurvedic herbal oils provide therapeutic benefits through massage. Warming sesame oil pacifies Vata when applied to joints, muscles and head. Cooling coconut oil calms aggravated Pitta when used externally. Nourishing bhringraj oil made with herbs promotes hair growth and scalp health. Heating mahanarayan oil relieves muscle soreness and stiffness. Antifungal neem oil clears skin and soothes irritation when applied topically. Herbalized oils optimize doshas through transdermal absorption.

Digestive herbs and formulas make excellent additions to a home apothecary. Hingashtak churna contains ginger, fennel, cumin and other carminative spices that reduce gas and bloating. Trikatu is a classic Ayurvedic pair of warming ginger, black pepper and pippli that ignites digestion. A teaspoon of shatavari, licorice or slippery elm powder mixed into warm milk at bedtime eases hyperacidity and ulcers. Gentle bitters like guduchi, neem or amalaki help optimize assimilation and elimination.

Several Ayurvedic herbs target mind-body balance for reducing anxiety, irritability and fatigue. Brahmi and jatamansi nourish and calm the nervous system, enhancing cognitive function. Tagara moderates sleep difficulties and emotional turbulence. Shankhpushpi sharpens intellect while relieving stress and depression. Ashwagandha counters exhaustion through energizing and adaptogenic actions. Tulsi, gotu kola and guggulu also stabilize mood and focus. Such mental tonics restore natural harmony and inner silence.

Respiratory formulas like sitopaladi churna make medicating at home convenient when needed. Containing cinnamon, licorice, cardamom and other warming herbs, sitopaladi thins mucus while fighting infection in lungs and sinuses. For dry cough or voice hoarseness, vasa churna with adhatoda, ginger and tulsi gives soothing lubrication. Antibacterial neem tablets purify against allergenic microbes. Kantakari, vasaka and pippali target obstinate Kapha congestion in airways. Keeping these respiratory aids on hand provides relief.

Several bitter and astringent Ayurvedic herbs help cleanse blood, lymph and microchannels for clear skin. Neem purifies heated, congested conditions causing acne or redness. Manjistha and guduchi reduce inflammation, discoloration and acne breakouts through lymphatic detoxification. Turmeric and gotu kola minimize wrinkles, scars and signs of aging. Aloe vera gel and rose petal paste pacify sensitive, irritated complexions. Using these herbs regularly restores collagen levels and glow.

Triphala and chywanaprash make excellent daily tonics for children that are gentler than harsh laxatives or antimicrobials. Ashwagandha and brahmi improve focus and calmness in attention deficit disorders. Slippery elm relieves GI irritation and reflux. Topical coconut oil soothes cradle cap and dermatitis when massaged into the scalp. Tulsi moderates coughs and colds while bolstering immunity. Under professional supervision, Ayurvedic herbs nurture children holistically.

The rejuvenative tonic chywanaprash provides antioxidant nutrition for elders and convalescents. Ashwagandha prevents exhaustion, weakness and cognitive decline. Bala and amalaki strengthen bones, immunity and vitality. Arjuna improves cardiovascular stamina and breathing difficulties. Milk with ginger, cardamom, ghee and honey nurtures emaciation and tissue depletion. Ayurvedic herbs administered judiciously sustain comfort, mobility and independence.

Herbal infusions and decoctions make preparing therapeutic teas simple. Cumin, coriander, fennel and cardamom decocted gently in water aids digestion. Tulsi, ginger and turmeric steeped as tea enhances circulation and antioxidation. Brahmi, jatamansi and nutmeg infused overnight calms the mind and nervous system. Acid-reducing teas use licorice, slippery elm, marshmallow root or shatavari. Customizing combinations targets different health goals effectively.

6.6 Ethical and Sustainable Sourcing:

Ayurveda's ancient herbal wisdom developed within a wholistic paradigm honoring the sacred interconnection between humanity and nature. As herbalism gained mainstream popularity globally, maintaining sustainability and integrity became imperative. Conscientious companies now prioritize environmental preservation, fair labor practices and preserving traditional knowledge when sourcing ingredients.

Seeking organically cultivated or ethically wild-harvested herbs supports their renewable abundance. Organic agriculture avoids synthetic fertilizers, pesticides and genetic modification that deplete ecosystems. Sustainable wild collection only takes what nature can replenish annually. Reforestation programs cultivating medicinal plants prevent over-foraging. Although more costly, such practices sustain plant vitality and availability.

Harvesting herbs at peak potency also enhances quality. The season, moon phase, time of day, climate and geography influence medicinal constituents. For example, sesame seeds picked in autumn retain the most warming energy to pacify Vata. Accounting for these nuances maximizes therapeutic potency beyond basic chemistry. Honoring traditional wisdom makes sustainability viable economically.

Fair trade certification ensures ethical treatment of farmers and wild collectors who supply herbs. A fair wage, safe working conditions, long-term contracts and ecological practices help communities thrive. By equitably sharing profits throughout the supply chain, herbalism empowers growers instead of exploiting them. We vote for justice with purchasing choices supporting ethical companies.

Seeking Ayurvedic herbs indigenous to their natural origin keeps traditional knowledge alive. Practitioners versed in local plant identification, harvesting and use pass wisdom down to communities. Cultivating regional herbs like tulsi, neem, turmeric and ginger also reduces environmental impacts of transport. Keeping botanical expertise decentralized sustains public access to herbal healing.

Chemical-free processing preserves the vital essence and biocompatibility of ingredients. Careful drying, milling and handling minimizes adulteration. While solvents and harsh extraction increase yields, natural enzymatic methods deliver a pure product. Ayurveda recognizes the inherent consciousness within plants that modern methods often destroy. Honoring natural synergy respects the sacrifice of harvested herbs.

Quality control testing transparency confirms identity, potency and purity. Batch analysis should verify active compounds and screen for contaminants. Good manufacturing practices standardize procedures for precision and cleanliness. Finished goods expiry testing by stability programs ensures consistent shelf life. Accountability to quality guidelines builds trust between consumers, practitioners and companies.

A Comprehensive Journey into Ayurvedic Healing

The holistic Ayurvedic paradigm respects plants as conscious beings who selflessly offer healing gifts. Relating to herbs as living entities exchanged through fair, compassionate commerce awakens their highest potential. Sustainable processes allow continued generosity from nature. By honoring Ayurveda's spiritual roots, herbalism creates harmony between people and the environment sustaining us all.Ayurveda provides an ecological model for herbalism that sustains both human health and the environment. By honoring the sanctity of plants and ethical commerce, this ancient wisdom offers solutions to modern sustainability challenges. Conscious companies now manifest Ayurveda's vision of unity between people and nature through their sourcing policies and practices.

Some reputable Ayurvedic brands like Banyan Botanicals, Maharishi Ayurveda and Organic India exemplify virtues like organic cultivation, fair trade, wildcrafting ethics and green manufacturing. We vote with our dollars to support businesses caring for communities and our Earth home. Seeking ingredients native to their natural habitat also reduces the environmental costs of global transport. Local crops grown regeneratively enhance regional self-reliance.

Education and activism help spread sustainable harvesting protocols in developing communities still learning such skills. Increased market demand that rewards ecologically sourced herbs incentivizes responsible practices. By setting standards for purity and ecological justice, Ayurveda progressively transforms the herbal industry.

Humanity owes immense gratitude to the ancient seers and Vaidyas whose wisdom gifted Ayurveda's herbal legacy to the world. Honoring those who came before while advancing knowledge for modern times demonstrates respect and care across generations. Each of us leaves a footprint upon the Earth. May we follow in the footsteps of illumined beings who walk in harmony with nature.

Combining technology with tradition also allows Ayurvedic herbalism to serve more people ethically. Updated textbooks share knowledge freely while the internet provides global access. Mindful adaptation is key, since modernization often leads to excessive industrialization at nature's expense. May we apply science compassionately, guided by holistic wisdom that protected these ways for millennia.

The essence of Ayurveda reminds us that lasting health comes not from exploiting nature, but appreciating interdependence between all life. Renewing this understanding in the modern world helps restore sustainable balance. Ayurveda's insights remain relevant because they illuminate laws of nature beyond time and place. By living in greater harmony with these universal principles, we bring wellbeing for all.

Chapter 7

Yoga and Meditation in Ayurveda

7.1 Yoga Asanas for the Doshas

Yoga and Ayurveda are sister sciences that both aim to promote optimal health and wellbeing. The former focuses on working with the body and breath to balance the body, mind, and spirit, while the latter provides guidance on diet, lifestyle, and herbal remedies to balance the doshas. When used together, yoga asanas and Ayurvedic wisdom offer a whole-person approach to healing and self-care.

In this chapter, we'll explore how to skillfully use yoga postures and sequences to balance each dosha and cultivate greater health. Though yoga is beneficial for everyone, when practiced in alignment with your unique mind-body type as described by Ayurveda, it can be especially transformative.

Those with a predominant Vata constitution tend to have light, thin frames and quick, energetic movements. When in balance, Vatas are creative, energetic, and flexible. When imbalanced, they can become stressed, anxious, and spacey. The key to balancing Vata is establishing a nurturing, grounding routine. Appropriate yoga asanas focus on stillness, strength, and stability.

Since Vata types tend to struggle with anxiety, overwhelmed nerves, and ""monkey mind,"" a regular practice of calm, soothing poses can work wonders. Forward bends such as Child's Pose, Wide-Legged Forward

A Comprehensive Journey into Ayurvedic Healing

Bend, and Standing Forward Bend give a sense of grounding. Backbends like Bridge Pose and Camel help counteract the hunching over that Vatas tend to do. And inversions including Downward Facing Dog, Legs Up the Wall, and Supported Shoulderstand have profoundly restorative benefits. Twists like Reclining Twist release mental tension and anxiety.

For Vatas, variety is important since they bore easily. Flow through Sun Salutations, exploring a wide range of asanas with mindfulness. Move at a moderate pace, avoiding overly-dynamic sequences that may deplete delicate Vata. The key is to stabilize, calm, and soothe. Focus on feeling each pose and breathing slowly. Follow yoga with restorative meditation. Overall, a well-rounded Vata practice balances effort and ease, movement and stillness, expansion and contraction.

Focused, intense, and organized, Pitta types have fiery determination and leadership skills. They thrive on challenge and achievement. But when imbalanced, they can overheat and turn critical, impatient, angry. Cooling, relaxing yoga asanas help balance excess Pitta and release simmering emotions.

Pittas benefit from a free-flowing, intuitive practice with emphasis on letting go, accepting imperfection, and not forcing things. Passive chest openers like Fish Pose and Supported Bridge Pose calm the emotions. Forward folds such as Wide-Legged Forward Bend and Standing Forward Bend induce surrender. Backbends like Camel and Wheel can help counteract Pitta's tendency to hunch forward over work. Twists release suppressed emotions held in the belly andAyurveda emphasizes nurturing awareness through mindfulness in all that we do. Beyond asana, establishing a formal meditation practice has profound benefits. Regular meditation tames the restless mind and heightens perception. Over time, we become more positively focused, composed, and resilient to life's ups and downs.

To cultivate a sustainable meditation habit, it helps immensely to set a consistent time for practice and link it to an existing daily routine. For instance, many find it effective to meditate first thing in the morning after brushing their teeth or mid-morning after breakfast. Ritualizing meditation in this way helps build it into your nervous system as a habit. Beginning with a small time investment like 5-10 minutes can make the practice feel accessible and manageable. It's easier to maintain meditating daily for short periods, and then the duration can slowly be increased over time.

Creating a sacred space conducive to meditation is also paramount. Set up your meditation area neatly and include objects that uplift you energetically. Bringing in elements from nature like flowers, crystals or small fountains can engage the senses. Using scent like essential oils and lighting candles sets a serene mood. Have cushions ready and ensure your spot is quiet and removed from disruption. By caring for your space, you demonstrate self-care and signal to your mind and body that meditation time is a revered ritual.

Starting with the simple practice of focusing on the breath and re-centering attention when it wanders lays the foundation. As you connect more deeply with the moment, insights about how to live with greater wisdom naturally arise. Releasing the accumulated stress of past and future thinking, you tap into newfound energy, creativity and inner peace. Like strengthening a muscle, the more meditation is practiced, the more natural awareness becomes. Gradually, meditation ceases to be limited to a sitting practice - its essence begins to infuse all of life.

7.2 Using Yoga for Healing and Balance

Yoga is an integral part of the Ayurvedic path to balance and wellbeing. The ancient science of yoga consists of both physical postures (asanas) as well as breath control (pranayama) and meditation techniques. According to Ayurveda, the regular practice of yoga benefits the body, mind, and spirit. It creates vitality, strengthens immunity, improves circulation, energizes digestion and promotes emotional balance. For these reasons, Ayurvedic physicians often prescribe specific yoga asanas tailored to each person's constitution and imbalance.

In this section, we will explore how to skillfully use yoga as a therapeutic tool based on your unique mind-body constitution. By practicing yoga asanas, pranayama and meditation geared toward your specific dosha, you can gently bring your system back into harmony. Vata types should focus on calming, centering poses while fiery Pitta types need cooling, relaxing asanas. For Kapha types prone to lethargy, stimulating active poses help counter stuck energy and inertia. With a balanced yoga practice, you'll feel both relaxed and energized.

We'll begin by looking at recommended yoga asanas for balancing each dosha. It's important to select poses that pacify your predominant dosha and to avoid poses that might aggravate it. For example, fast-paced repetitive flows would disturb sensitive Vata but be fine for sluggish Kapha. Let's explore the best asanas for finding doshic balance.

For Vata types, key asanas are those that promote grounding, stability and stillness. Asanas that strengthen the lower body, open the hips and reinforce posture are excellent. Poses like Mountain Pose, Tree Pose, Triangle Pose and Wide-Legged Forward Fold calm restless Vata. Inversions like Downward Facing Dog, Legs Up the Wall and Supported Shoulder Stand calm the overactive mind. Since Vata is cold and dry, warming nourishing poses help balance it. Planks, Chaturangas, Bridge Pose and Child's Pose generate internal heat. Restorative poses like Reclining Bound Angle and Supported Fish help settle the racing Vata mind. Practicing at the same time daily is important for Vata and flowing slowly with focus.

Pitta types need cooling, relaxing asanas to reduce excess fire and intensity. Poses like Moon Salutations, Wide-Angle Seated Forward

Bend, Bound Angle and Reclining Twist help calm fiery Pitta. Passive chest openers like Sphinx, Camel and Fish give expansion without heat. Shoulder stand inversions and forward folds promote cooling. Since Pitta can be competitive, it's best to practice without judgement and avoid heated, fast classes. Morning practice is ideal as Kapha dosha predominates then. Flowing slowly with long holds balances intensity. Pitta benefits from practicing outdoors or in cool rooms. Moon salutations, goddess and standing postures satisfy Pitta's need for activity without overheating.

For Kapha doshas, asanas that generate heat, stimulate and promote lightness are best. Warming sun salutations, active backbends like Locust, Bow and Camel and strength-builders like Side Plank and Four-Limbed Staff Pose counter heavy Kapha. Standing poses that require balance like Tree, Eagle, Dancer and Extended Hand to Big Toe challenge sluggish Kapha. Chest-openers, twists and core strengtheners get energy moving. Since Kapha accumulation can lead to weight gain, vinyasas, Sun Salutations and active flow help trim excess. Allowing the breath to move freely prevents stagnation. Practicing in the later afternoon when Kapha builds up is beneficial. Focusing on lightness and dynamism keeps heavy Kapha from dragging the energy down.

In addition to tailoring asanas to your doshic makeup, Ayurveda offers guidance on using yoga therapeutically for healing and balance. Yogic practices can pacify specific imbalanced doshas and gently guide them back into harmony. For example, to calm excess Vata, focus on restorative poses. Forward folds, gentle twists, Supported Bridge and Bound Angle reduce overwhelm. Placing a sandbag on the low belly while practicing Savasana can reassure ungrounded Vata.

Hot fiery Pitta is balanced by passive chest openers, shoulder stand and forward bends. Practicing Chandra Namaskar or Moon Salutations has a cooling effect. Bound Angle Pose, Upavistha Konasana straddles and wide-legged folds calm the intensity. Splashing cool water on the face and neck after practice reduces heat. Chanting tones down excessive speech and mental activity.

For heavy, sluggish Kapha, active heating practices invigorate. Backbends open the chest to counter stuck energy. Arm balances and core work build strength and stamina. Surya Namaskar generates inner fire to burn accumulations. Sama Vritti pranayama's equal exhale/inhale ratio provides energetic balance. Kapalabhati and Bhastrika clear stagnation. Focusing on the invigorating effects of poses keeps practice lively.In addition to asanas, pranayama breathing practices also balance the doshas in Ayurvedic yoga. Through controlled breathing, we can instill qualities lacking in our constitutions. Cooling breaths benefit fiery Pitta while warming breaths help cold Vata and Kapha. Deep belly breaths stimulate sluggish systems. Alternate nostril breathing calms the mind. By matching pranayama to your needs, you restore equilibrium.

Vata types need grounding breaths like Ujjayi, which creates a soothing ocean sound. Inhaling and exhaling through the nose calms the nervous system. Low-tone Om chanting vibrating the chest relaxes the body. Deep three-part Yogic breathing with long exhales aides relaxation. Warming solar plexus Bastrika energizes without overwhelming sensitive Vata. Cooling lunar breaths should be avoided. A short 6-8 round Kapalabhati energizes and dispels air.

For Pitta, the key is cooling, relaxing pranayama. Alternate nostril breathing soothes the mind and nervous system. Cooling Sitali and Sitkari, involving curling the tongue, calms excess heat. Victorious Breath balances the solar and lunar energies. Chandrabhedana cools the emotions through left nostril breathing. Sheetali hissing breath releases steam. Avoiding forced, rapid breathing prevents friction. Short rounds of warming breaths heat up the body gradually.

Kapha types need stimulating, heating breaths like warming Bhastrika and its variations. Kapalabhati's pumping action builds heat and moves stagnation. Ujjayi builds internal fire and dispels inertia. Back-of-throat Ujjayi creates warmth. Strong three-part Yogic breathing provides energetic lift. Alternate nostril breathing balances solar/lunar channels. Sama Vritti's equal inhale and exhale ratio creates equilibrium. Allowing the exhales to remain long and smooth prevents stagnation.

Moving beyond asana and pranayama, meditation is equally essential in Ayurvedic yoga for relaxing the mind and soothing the nervous system. By training the mind to become Still through silent meditation, we contact our inner source of peace and pure Awareness. When practiced regularly, meditation profoundly calms Vata anxiety, Pitta irritation and Kapha mental fog. Let's explore effective meditation techniques for each mind-body type.

Vata meditators benefit from grounded, calming techniques to still their monkey minds. Following the breath trains wandering Vata awareness to focus gently on sensation. Mantra repetition gives an auditory anchor to flighty Vata. Guided meditations provide needed structure. Warming solar plexus focus grounds ungrounded Vata. Eyes-closed channels energy inward and settles the system. Starting with brief sessions prevents overwhelm. Silently counting exhales relaxes thinking minds.

For intense Pitta, passive open monitoring meditation helps release steam buildup. Cooling moon imagery and chants redirect fiery emotions. Metta loving-kindness meditation develops compassion and acceptance. Candle-gazing anchors the senses. Eyes-slightly-open meditations allow the mind to softly fall inward. Focusing on the interval between thoughts takes the heat off mental angst. Open sky or ocean visualizations give spaciousness. Moving meditations like Tai Chi settle rajasic Pitta.

Kapha types need active, warming meditations to energize the body and mind. Visualizing flames and repeating stimulating seed mantras like ""Om Hrim"" build internal fire. Back-of-throat Ujjayi with silent mantra energizes dullness. Walking meditation and sustained sky gazing burn mental fog. Dynamic forms like Kinhin provide missing motion. Silently repeating affirmations invokes clarity and inspiration. Eyes-open meditations take advantage of Kapha's alertness. Chanting rhythmical mantras with mridanga beats dispels inertia.

Beyond foundational meditation instructions, developing a balanced personal practice is key in Ayurvedic yoga. Observe when your mind naturally turns inward, then set this time aside for practice. Create a sacred space that elicits relaxation and devotion. Find a comfortable posture that embodies alertness and ease. Set reasonable practice lengths and gradually increase. Integrate all aspects of 8-limbed yoga from ethics to meditation. Allow practice to nourish spiritual connection. Pursue a steady practice with patience and non-striving. Let yoga support your journey toward vibrant health, mental clarity and inner peace.

The beauty of yoga's 8 limbs is their capacity to holistically uplift body, mind and spirit. Asana and pranayama balance the physical forces while Pratyhara sensory withdrawal and Dharana concentration prepare for meditation. As we'll explore in the next section, adding mantra and visualization further nourishes our inner terrain. Ultimately yoga takes us beyond the physical to experience the sacred ground of our being. With devoted practice, we ride the breath into the silent expansive space that connects us all as One.

7.3 Establishing a Meditation Practice

In the yogic tradition, meditation is considered an essential practice for calming the fluctuations of the mind and perceiving our innate spiritual nature. Regular meditation confers countless benefits: lowering stress, reducing anxiety and depression, improving focus and cognitive function, promoting emotional resilience and fostering a sense of inner peace. From an Ayurvedic perspective, a suitably tailored meditation practice balances the doshas and creates mental, emotional and physical harmony.

As we've explored, yoga and Ayurveda are sister sciences focused on optimal health and spiritual awakening. Meditation creates the mental stillness and discernment required to experience our divine eternal essence beyond our temporary thoughts and emotions. By training the mind through spiritual practice, we can undo our conditioning and access pure consciousness. In this section, we'll look at establishing a regular meditation routine and explore techniques for quieting the content of the mind to abide as silent witnessing awareness.

To begin a meditation practice, set aside time each morning before obligations arise. Wake up 20-30 minutes early and complete bathroom rituals and self-care to create space for undisturbed practice. Prepare your space by lighting a candle, playing soft instrumental music or reciting an opening prayer. Sit comfortably with a straight spine; you can use cushions to support the posture. Commit to a reasonable duration starting with 5-10 minutes and increasing weekly. Use a phone or timer so you needn't break focus to check the clock. Resolve to practice regularly without expectations or judgements.

For beginners, focus on anchoring awareness in the present moment. You can use the breath, a mantra or a visual object as the anchor. Place your attention softly on the sensation of inhaling and exhaling. When the mind wanders, gently return to the breath. You can silently count ""one"" on the inhale, ""two"" on the exhale. Alternatively, repeat a mantra like ""Om"" coordinating with the breath. Another option is to gaze at a candle flame or a meaningful image, continually refocusing when distracted. The key is concentrating awareness while maintaining a relaxed, receptive attitude.

It's helpful to sit upright on the front edge of a chair or cushion, allowing the spine to elongate. Let your chin tuck slightly and the crown of the head lift toward the sky. Rest your palms face up on the thighs or in the lap. Soften the gaze downward or close the eyes. Relax the muscles of the face, shoulders and abdomen. Either keep the mouth closed and breathe through the nose or allow the lips to part slightly. Let the breath flow effortlessly without forcing. Allow your focus to ride the waves of the inhalation and exhalation.

When thoughts inevitably arise, don't resist or suppress them forcefully. Rather than struggling with the thought stream, practice observing thoughts with neutral detachment. Notice how thoughts form, peak in intensity, then dissolve back into the void. Try labeling thoughts "planning," "judging," "doubting" without getting emotionally involved in their content. Like clouds passing through the sky, let thoughts drift by without clinging. Keep returning to the breath or mantra anchor with patient attention. Mindfulness of the present moment continually reorients awareness from thoughts to pure perception.

As your ability to concentrate improves through regular practice, you can experiment with different types of meditation geared toward your doshic makeup. Vata types benefit from mantra repetition and gentle guided visualizations. Pittas do well observing the intervals between thoughts. Kaphas thrive with candle gazing or silence/insight techniques. Tailoring the approach helps calm or stimulate specific doshas. Always end by dedicating the merits of your practice toward alleviating others' suffering. Establishing this beneficial ritual nourishes body, mind and spirit.

Proper preparation before meditation is key. It's best to practice on an empty but not hungry stomach to minimize digestive discomfort. You may elect to practice meditation right upon awakening or an hour or so after breakfast. Drink some warm water to moisten the palette if you intend to repeat mantras. Practice proper elimination before sitting to avoid restless urgency. Set reasonable goals for practice duration and increase the time week by week. Practicing meditation at the same time daily strengthens commitment through routine.Once you've laid the foundation, you can begin exploring specific meditation techniques tailored to balance the doshas. Cooling meditations calm fiery Pitta while warming practices enliven cold Kapha and Vata. We'll look at effective approaches for each mind-body type.

For Vata, mantra repetition is calming and focusing. Chanting "Om" while following the breath anchors the airy Vata mind. Humming deeply in the throat creates soothing vibrations. Repeating positive affirmations instills confidence and optimism. Guided meditations provide needed structure for Vata's variable attention. Visualizing nurturing images like an ocean or garden stills the active intellect. Attending to sensations in the lower body and pelvic floor grounds ungrounded Vata.

Pitta benefits from open monitoring and insight practices. Observing the spaces between thoughts releases steam pressure. Noting how anger and irritation arise and fade builds non-reactivity. Imagining the mind as the vast open sky places awareness beyond content. Focusing on the heart center results in compassion and forgiveness. Cooling moon and water visualizations balance heat. Reminding oneself "thoughts aren't facts" reduces mental grasping. Allowing the mind's activity to self-liberate creates space.

For Kapha, active meditations counter inertia and stagnation. Visualizing brilliant light invokes mental clarity and inspiration. Repeating "Om Hrim" while following the breath builds internal fire. Kapalabhati and Bhastrika pranayamas energize before meditation. Sky gazing cues upward energy flow. Walking meditation and yoga melt heaviness. Noting when the mind gets drowsy and dull keeps one alert. Silently affirming "I am pure consciousness" awakens presence. Keeping the eyes open avoids grogginess.

In addition to basic techniques, integrating mantra and imagery further enlivens meditation. Mantras are empowered syllables that tune consciousness to particular energies. Visualizations channel the mind's power to visualize desired states. We'll explore potent mantras and images for uplifting the doshas.

Seed mantras like Om Namah Shivaya invoke divine primordial energies. Chanting Om Tryambakam Yajamahe enlivens spiritual fire for purification. Om Mani Padme Hum connects to compassion and wisdom. Lam, Vam, Ram, Yam, Ham seed mantras align with the elements. Mantras can be repeated aloud, whispered or mentally. Creative visualizations build new neural patterns. Seeing oneself immersed in golden light releases negativity. Imagining breathing light into the heart center heals emotional pain. Visualizing the spiritual eye radiating at the brow point awakens intuition.

It's also helpful to integrate meditation into daily activities through mindfulness and witnessing awareness. While brushing your teeth or washing dishes, follow the sensations mindfully. Pause occasionally to observe the space between thoughts. Practice listening without judgment in conversations. Appreciate the taste and textures of meals with full engagement. Move through asana practice consciously uniting breath, body and mind. Carry meditative awareness into all activities.

As your practice deepens, you may experience meditative absorption, insight into the nature of reality or sacred spiritual states. Allow these to unfold organically without attachment. Avoid judging progress or comparing yourself to others. Let go of expectations for special experiences. Practice with patience, perseverance and trust in your inner wisdom. Meditation ripens like fruit in its own time. Stay focused on consistency rather than achievement. Keep orienting from ego toward spirit.

By establishing a regular meditation ritual, you take the first steps on the journey from a noisy mind to inner stillness. Gradually mental chatter diminishes and awareness becomes anchored in the eternal present. You recognize the conditioned self as temporary and the infinite silent Self as your true nature. Each moment of practice brings you closer to abiding peace, joy and oneness. Pursue your path with courage, humor and self-compassion.

7.4 Meditation Techniques for Beginners

As a meditation beginner, it's helpful to start with basic techniques that train concentration and anchor awareness in the present moment. We'll explore introductory practices suitable for each dosha to establish a foundation. Mastering meditation takes time and consistency. By starting simple, you can progressively deepen your practice over months and years.

For those new to meditation, focusing on the breath is an excellent way to steady the mind. Sit comfortably and turn your attention to the flow of your inhaling and exhaling. Notice where you feel the breath most prominently, perhaps in the rise and fall of the chest or abdominal area. Allow your focus to rest gently on each inhalation and exhalation without controlling the breath in any way. When thoughts pull your attention away, patiently return to the sensation of breathing.

This simple mindfulness of breathing develops concentration and relaxes both mind and body. It also anchors awareness in the present, helping counteract rumination about the past and future. As you become distracted less frequently, you'll experience longer periods of relaxed focus between thoughts. With regular practice, the mind becomes lucid, calm and centered.

Another foundational technique is silently repeating a mantra in rhythm with the breath. Mantras are spiritually efficacious syllables that create particular vibrational effects in consciousness. For calming the mind, the mantra "Om" is excellent. As you inhale, mentally repeat "Om" and as you exhale, repeat "Om" again. This anchors the attention and introduces a devotional mood. Alternatively, you can synchronize mantras like "Sat Nam" with walking or household chores.

If you're very visually oriented, candle gazing can be centering. Sit comfortably Before a lit candle placed at eye level. Softly focus your gaze on the flame, maintaining a passive relaxed attention. When thoughts or distractions arise, gently return your gaze to the flame. Allow the flickering light to absorb your awareness. Observe the luminous quality of the flame until it fills your field of vision. This concentrates the mind through a visual focal point.

For those drawn to devotional practice, imagining holy images or teachers can anchor the meditation. Hold the sacred image clearly in your mind's eye, noticing details of color, light and perspective. If your attention drifts, visualize the image again. The image may change organically or you may remain with a single image for the entire meditation. Allow feelings of inspiration, gratitude or loving connection to arise. This anchors awareness through visualization and devotion.

If you feel sleepy or sluggish during meditation, try keeping your eyes slightly open. Rather than fully closing the eyes, lower your eyelids to about half mast. Allow your gaze to fall softly downward a few feet in front of you. With eyes open just enough to let in light, less melatonin is produced so you'll feel more alert. Relax the eyes while keeping the optic muscles engaged.

For energetic types who get restless with too much stillness, light yoga asanas just before meditation can help calm and focus the mind. A few standing postures like Warrior and extended lateral stretches help release excess energy. Forward bends counter mental agitation. Supine poses like Savasana provide needed tranquility. Move through a brief, balancing sequence before sitting quietly.

These basic techniques give you a solid foundation to begin reorienting from thinking toward silent presence. At first the mind will be quite active and concentration fluctuating. With regular patient practice, you'll progress through stages from distraction to sustained mental clarity. Proceed with curiosity, humor and gratitude for each step forward on the journey within.Once you've developed basic competence through foundational practices, you'll be ready to try other time-tested meditation techniques for calming or stimulating specific doshas. Tailoring the approach to your mind-body type enhances the benefits. We'll explore fruitful practices for balancing Vata, Pitta and Kapha.

To calm busy Vata minds, guided meditations provide needed structure. Close your eyes and listen to a soothing voice that lead you step-by-step into relaxation. Let the guidance carry your awareness through imagery of walking down steps into a serene garden or floating on a gentle river. Allow any emotions, memories or sensations to arise. Focused, slower-paced mantra repetition also engages restless Vata.

For intense, fiery Pitta, open monitoring is effective. Rather than fixating on an object like the breath, Pitta benefits from choiceless observation of the present moment. Notice sights, smells, sounds and bodily sensations without judgment. Watch the intervals between thoughts. Don't block emotions but view them impartially as they rise and subside. This releases steam from the mind without suppression.

To energize calm Kapha, try gazing meditation. Focus your eyes softly on the flame of a candle, shifting your gaze periodically to different parts of the flame. This concentration charges the mind and senses without being overly stimulating. Alternatively, allow the eyes to gaze upwards into imaginary space. Avoid closing the eyes entirely to prevent sluggishness.

Once you've practiced basic techniques long enough to still and focus the mind, you can experiment with more advanced nondual meditation.

Rather than concentrating on an object like the breath or an image, turn your attention upon itself. Observe the awareness which is aware of thoughts. Sense the space in which thoughts come and go. Abide as a timeless presence behind the mind. Rest in the silent witness that perceives all experience. This points toward your true nature beyond all objects.

To further calm and center the mind, mindfulness during everyday activities brings meditative presence into mundane tasks. While washing dishes, attend fully to the tactile sensations, movements and sounds. Chew slowly when eating, noticing tastes and textures. Brush your teeth consciously feeling your arm move and the bristles cleaning. This trains concentration amidst daily life.

Seeking spiritual guidance can also deepen your understanding through wisdom transmitted from teacher to student. Attend retreats or meditation workshops to absorb elevated energy. Study classic texts like the Yoga Sutras and Tao Te Ching. Contemplate paradoxical Zen koans which confound conceptual thinking. Discourse with advanced practitioners who've realized expanded consciousness. Allow teachings to permeate your awareness.

As your practice matures, you'll alternate effortlessly between "waves" of concentration and "waves" of witnessing awareness. Moments of focused attention on objects like mantras or the breath will be interspersed with open spacious observation. Your meditation may become transconceptual and luminous. These fruits naturally arise through sustained sincere practice. Stay on your cushion and truth will unfold in its own time!

7.5 Mantras and Visualizations

In yogic and Vedic traditions, mantras are sacred syllables imbued with spiritual power. Chanting mantras during meditation engages the mind and heart, creating beneficial vibrations. Similarly, creative visualization harnesses the imagination's capacity to produce healing mental states. Combining mantra repetition with vivid imagery multiplies the effects. In this section, we'll explore potent mantras and visuals for uplifting body, mind and spirit.

"Om" is the primordial sound from which all creation springs. Chanting Om aligns our individual consciousness with the macrocosmic infinite consciousness. It creates harmony between the physical, subtle and causal bodies. Om is the foremost mantra for centering awareness and dissolving thoughts into peaceful tranquility. Repeat it audibly first, then gradually inwardly. Allow the resonances to ripple through mind and body.

The mantra "Om Namah Shivaya" translates as "I bow to the inner Self." It invokes the higher wisdom within each person that is one with universal spirit. Shiva represents pure undifferentiated awareness beyond form. Chanting this mantra installs our identity in limitless consciousness rather than the limited body-mind. It creates devotion, humility and joy.

"Om Mani Padme Hum" is the mantra of compassion. Mani means "jewel" while Padme represents the "lotus flower." Our innate compassion and wisdom are precious jewels residing within the lotus of consciousness. Repeating this mantra while imagining a glowing gem within a lotus opens our capacity for love, empathy and insight. It awakens our Buddha nature.

The mantra "Om Tryambakam Yajamahe" invokes Shiva in his three-eyed form representing the Trinity of creation, preservation and destruction. This omnipotent, omniscient, omnipresent aspect of the Divine governs the cycles of manifestation. Chanting benefits spiritual progress, prosperity and blessing.

A Comprehensive Journey into Ayurvedic Healing

The mantra "Om Gam Ganapataye Namaha" invokes Ganesh, the elephant-headed deity who removes obstacles and confers wisdom. Gam signifies the secret mantra bringing Ganesh's blessings upon the chanter. Visualizing Ganesh's form and chanting his mantra before endeavors ushers in success. Obstacles dissolve and right action flows effortlessly.

These seed mantras align consciousness with particular archetypal energies of the Divine. Alternatively, one can silently repeat affirmations, prayers or passages from wisdom writings. Choose uplifting words radiating qualities you aspire towards like compassion, strength, wisdom, equanimity and devotion.

In addition to sounding sacred syllables vocally or mentally, adding visualizations maximizes the effects. Imagine absorbing illuminating rays of sunlight, moonlight or starlight. Repeat cleansing mantras while envisioning negativity dissolving into rainbow light. Picture loved ones surrounded by golden halos of protection. See yourself effortlessly embodying your highest values.

The chakras, or energy centers along the spine, have related colors, elements and mantras we can visualize to balance their functioning. For example, imagine shining an emerald green light and repeating "Om Yum" to activate the heart chakra. Chant "Om Vum" while visualizing sapphire blue to open the throat. Creatively use chakra correspondences.Contemplating elevating passages from scriptures also directs the mind positively. Read a verse, reflect upon it, then orient awareness toward its meaning. This engages the intellect in constructive rumination rather than unhelpful thinking. Or receive a teaching from your spiritual mentor inwardly through imagination. Ask their wisdom mind to permeate your own.

Once you've gained proficiency with foundational practices, visualization becomes effortless. Imagine scenes, teachers, deities, symbols or energy centers spontaneously without clinging. First use volition and intention to create detailed inner visuals. Then allow them to organically arise like dreams. Practice open receptivity to guidance from higher aspects of your being.

See your body as hollow, filled with shimmering rainbow light. Picture negativity as dark sticky tar leaving through your feet. Invent visual analogies - stagnant energy as sludge becoming purified into flowing water. Create mini-movies of resolving conflicts peacefully or accomplishing goals. Harness your imagination's power to produce positive mental states.

Use images, memories or sensations that elicit particular emotions - a loved one for compassion, warmth of sun for joy, favorite retreat for serenity. Or work backward from desired emotions to visuals that induce them. Does a starry sky prompt awe? Ocean waves peace? Cherry blossom's ephemeral beauty? Let inner scenery lead to insight.

 notice which mantras resonate in your own consciousness. Experiment with different seed syllables and passages to discern which energize, pacify or uplift you. Chant them as you engage in activities - walking, cooking, cleaning. Find mantras which serve as touchstones when you need centering, protection or inspiration. Let them become genuine spiritual companions.

While formal mantra meditation has great benefits, casual mantra repetition also focuses the mind incrementally. Waiting in line at the store, silently repeat "I am patient." Feeling tense, mentally chant "I am calm." mantras repattern neural pathways to manifest their qualities. They serve as affirmations rewriting limiting beliefs. With creativity and sincerity, mantras illuminate consciousness.

Don't underestimate the potency of humble mantras like "Thank you," "I forgive," "Help me." In moments of anger or grief, chanting "Om" defuses reactivity. When receiving generosity, mentally intone "I accept gratefully." Headed into a challenge, repeat "I am courageous" to enlist spiritual forces on your side. Mantras morph energy into vibrations consonant with your soul.

By engaging concentrated imagination to manifest elevated mental states, mantra and visualization practices profoundly transform awareness. What we mentally repeat and envision, we become. Combining sacred sound with luminous imagery aligns limited self with cosmic infinite Self. Start now empowering your path toward peace, wisdom and wholeness through creative use of mantra and visualization.

7.6 Developing a Personalized Practice

While we've explored many beneficial meditation techniques, developing an integrated personal practice optimizes the benefits over time. Tailor your approach to your unique mind-body makeup, life circumstances and evolving spiritual needs. Be creative and responsive in shaping a practice that serves your growth.

Begin by contemplating your intention for practice. Are you seeking stress relief, self-understanding, spiritual connection, worldly detachment? Observe when your energy and focus naturally turn inward, then schedule this time for meditation. Start with short sessions of 10-15 minutes and extend them progressively.

Try a variety of techniques without attachment to any. Mindfulness, mantra, guided imagery, breathwork, insight and nondual meditations all have value. Rotate through or combine approaches in synergy. For example, alternate watching the breath then silently repeating affirmations. Over months and years, discern what meditation forms nourish you most.

While structure can help establish a habit, don't become rigid in practice. Adjust techniques, duration and frequency based on your level of experience and changing life demands. If you feel bored or agitated, switch to a different method. If you're very busy, even a few minutes meditating before bed helps. Stay responsive.

Pay attention to your energetic cycles through the day. Kapha types may benefit most from meditating early before heaviness sets in. Pitta can practice at sunrise when Kapha predominates. Vata should avoid late night meditation which might disturb sleep. Find your optimal times.

The key is sticking with your practice through ups and downs. Don't judge slow progress or dry periods - they're natural. Be gentle with yourself when the mind is restless. Avoid future goals - stay immersed in the present. Have patience as meditation unfolds gradually through sustained practice over months and years.

Creatively adapt meditation to your circumstances. Householders can practice amidst the sounds of family life. Use commute time for breath counting. While in bed awaiting sleep, repeat mantras. Those with physical limitations can meditate lying down. Stay open and flexible.

For added inspiration, support your practice through spiritual community and study. Attend retreats, listen to talks, reflect on writings that uplift your understanding. Stay connected to the larger context for your personal journey. Wisdom shared helps anchor insights.

Evaluate periodically if you've become unbalanced or attached. Too much silence can dull the senses for active types. Excess visualization may overstimulate the mind. Check that nondual meditation isn't bypassing needed therapeutic work. Adjust as required.

Most importantly, orient your practice toward spiritual freedom rather than self-improvement. Meditation is about shining the light of awareness on the ego's limitations, not fortifying them. With dedicated practice, you will move beyond seeking special experiences toward abiding peace.

By experimenting, evaluating and adjusting based on your temperament and phase of growth, you'll develop a fluid, integrated meditation practice. Support your inner journey with spiritual community, study and service. Your path will unfold beautifully as you persist with humility and devotion.In addition to formal seated meditation, integrating mindfulness throughout your daily life is beneficial. Perform routine tasks consciously, with full engagement of the senses. Notice the sights, textures, smells and sounds of cooking, washing, and commuting. Bring awareness fully into each activity.

Practice mindfulness during interpersonal interactions. Listen attentively without anticipating your response. Pause before speaking to check your emotional state. Discern whether reactions are appropriate or exaggerated. Communicate skillfully from calm wisdom.

Notice emotional triggers that lead to hurtful speech or conduct. Observe how destructive states like anger or fear arise and fabricate stories. Don't suppress feelings, but view them with detachment. This reduces habitual reactivity.

Try meditating while walking in nature. Focus all senses on your surroundings - bird songs, breeze on your skin, scent of flowers. Or enjoy a mindful silent meal. Appreciate the presentation, aroma, flavor and textures of each bite as if eating this food for the first time.

Incorporate mindfulness of your social media use and web surfing. Periodically ask ""is this content uplifting or wasting my time?"" Consciously limit scrolling when it no longer adds value. Apply meditation to wisely manage the barrage of technology.

Practice observing your thoughts, emotions and body sensations with impartial detachment. Witness anger without believing its narrative or acting unskillfully. Watch fear arise and dissipate without identifying with it. See thoughts as passing mental events rather than truth.

When you notice yourself feeling stuck in obsessive mental loops, pause and turn attention to your breathing or physical environment. This interrupts rumination and re-grounds your perspective. Release obsessive fixation through mindful reorientation to the present.

Before reacting to difficult people, pause to access your inner wisdom. Silently ask, "What would be the most skillful response here - for myself and others?" Follow the guidance that arises from your depths. This replaces reaction with conscious response.

As you progress, begin witnessing the witness itself. Observe the silent presence of awareness which perceives all changing phenomena. Abide as the stillness behind the movement of thoughts. Rest in timeless Being.

Evaluate your actions - are they serving ego or spirit? Align behaviors with your deepest values, not egoic desires. Let go of unhelpful habits with patience. Meditate on how your faults stem from ignorance rather than malice. This transforms character over time.

By infusing your days with meditative presence, you directly apply spiritual principles to optimizing health and relations. Mindfulness enhances productivity by reducing distraction. Equanimity stabilizes moods. Insight pierces delusion. Compassion heals conflict. Your growth benefits all.

Chapter 8

Ayurvedic Approaches to Common Ailments

8.1 Remedies for Digestive Issues

Ayurveda offers a wealth of natural remedies for improving digestion and eliminating ama, or toxins, from the gastrointestinal tract. Poor digestion leads to the accumulation of undigested food material called "ama" which clogs the channels of the body and leads to disease. By enhancing agni (digestive fire) and removing obstructions, Ayurvedic treatments restore balance and nourish the entire system.

The key elements for optimal digestion are strong agni, efficient elimination, lubricated intestines, and calm emotional state. When agni is impaired, food isn't broken down properly, leading to fermentation, gas and bloating. Weak elimination results in stagnant waste and constipation. Dry intestines disturb peristaltic action and cause discomfort. Stress inhibits digestion. Let's explore time-tested Ayurvedic therapies to remedy all these and promote smooth digestion.

Before eating, sip warm water with a pinch of rock salt and ginger, lime juice or mint to stimulate digestive juices. Trying resting your left hand over your navel and massaging gently as you slowly drink some warm water. This activates the samana vayu governing digestion.

Sip fresh ginger tea made with sliced ginger root steeped in hot water before meals. Ginger improves agni without aggravating pitta. You can add a pinch of rock salt and lime juice. For heavy kapha types, mix in a little honey and lemon. This classic tea stimulates digestion and removes ama.

Take trikatu, a digestive formula containing ginger, black pepper and pippali, 5-10 minutes before eating. This heating combination kindles agni, burns up excess kapha and breaks down ama. Triphala, a traditional formula of three fruits, scrapes away toxins and improves elimination.

Eat your largest meal at lunch when digestion is strongest. Have a light warm breakfast and small early dinner. Wait until the previous meal has been digested before eating more food. Avoid cold, raw foods which dampen agni. Include freshly grated ginger in cooking.

After meals, chew a small piece of ginger with a pinch of salt to promote digestion. Sip peppermint, cumin, coriander or fennel tea to ease bloating and gas. Go for a short walk to circulate nutrients and enhance elimination. Rest in Vajrasana pose applying gentle pressure on the lower abdomen.

Observe proper food combining - avoid mixing fruit with other foods or eating multiple protein sources together. Favor cooked seasonal foods over raw salads. Minimize iced beverages which freeze agni. Adopting Ayurvedic dietary principles optimizes digestion.

Release suppressed emotions like fear, anger and grief which inhibit digestion. Practice yoga asanas that liberate feelings and energize the pelvis and abdomen. Learn healthy ways to identify and express your emotions for digestive harmony. Breathe deeply into the belly.

Chew your food thoroughly until it becomes almost liquid. This lightens the digestive load. Relax the belly and avoid eating while upset. Sip warm water with meals. These habits reduce anxiety that blocks digestion. Eat peacefully without multitasking for easeful assimilation.

If you feel acute indigestion, drink a cup of hot water with 10 drops of ginger-infused honey and a squeeze of lemon. The ginger and lemon stimulate agni while the honey coats and soothes the gut lining. For gas pains, chew toasted cumin, fennel or caraway seeds.

Sensitive Vata types should favor warm, cooked foods with healthy oils and mild spices. Fiery Pitta types need cooling foods like cucumber, bitter greens and coconut. Heavy Kapha types require light, drying and warming foods cooked with stimulating spices. Tailor diet to support your unique digestion.

By tuning in to your body's signals, you can discern which foods truly agree with you. Notice symptoms of indigestion like belching, bloating or heaviness after eating. Avoid foods that repeatedly cause these issues. Keep a food diary to identify offenders.If constipation is an issue, drink a glass of warm milk with ghee before bedtime. This lubricates the intestines and draws water into the colon. Flax, chia and psyllium seeds also add needed bulk. Avoid cold, raw, dry foods that create hard stools. Gentle yoga twists and inverted poses encourage elimination.

Triphala is the most revered Ayurvedic formula for gently loosening stools while detoxifying the GI tract. Take 1/2 to 1 teaspoon daily at night with warm water. For acute constipation, soak 2-4 tablespoons overnight in water and drink in the morning.

Massaging the lower abdomen in circular clockwise motions with warm sesame oil helps stimulate peristalsis. Follow with warm castor oil packs over the abdomen to relieve constipation. Alternating hot and cold hip baths improves circulation in the pelvis.

Practice dry-brushing the skin before bathing to open elimination channels. Use a natural bristle brush and brush the entire body moving from the extremities inward. Sip warm water throughout the day to maintain hydration. Adequate water intake prevents wastes from drying and sticking.

Fasting gives the digestive organs a chance to rest and cleanses the body of ama. For kapha types especially, a liquid mono-diet of kitchari or fresh juices 1-2 days a week lightens the system. Consult your practitioner before extended water or juice fasts.

Rasayana herbs like amlaki, guduchi, shatavari and ashwagandha rejuvenate the digestive tissues and strengthen agni long-term. Take Chyawanprash jam, an Ayurvedic tonic containing amlaki, before meals. The wide array of herbs nourish all tissue layers.

Cultivating awareness through yoga and meditation heals imbalances at their root. Stress and suppressed emotions disturb digestion over time. Learn to address issues skillfully. Let go of negative patterns through spiritual practices. Embody the peaceful joy of your true nature.

When acute digestive distress occurs, sip warm water with lemon juice and raw honey. Avoid solid food until symptoms resolve. Once feeling better, eat a light kitchari or broth soup. Gradual introduce solid foods starting with rice, quinoa and cooked vegetables.

During illness, the body's wisdom guides you to rest and fast temporarily. Heed those signals. Do not override them and force yourself to eat while digestion is compromised. With a day of rest and liquids, agni usually rebounds.

Certain yoga postures aid elimination when needed. Forward bends massage the organs while twists wring out toxins. Inverted poses encourage venous blood flow. Stretches like Bow and Bridge activate the pelvic floor. Practice gently, honoring your body's signals.

By attentively observing digestion's cues and responding with Ayurvedic wisdom, you can optimize this vital process. Keep agni stoked through proper diet, emotions and self-care. Cleanse regularly to prevent ama accumulation. Digestion affects every cell - make it a priority in your holistic self-care.

8.2 Managing Pain and Inflammation

Ayurveda offers a wealth of natural anti-inflammatory therapies to alleviate pain and swelling in the body. By reducing inflammatory compounds, improving circulation and removing blockages, these remedies restore the free flow of prana, balance the doshas and relieve discomfort.

Inflammation, or heat and swelling in tissues, arises from aggravated Pitta dosha. Pitta governs metabolism, digestion and immunity in the body. When disturbed by poor diet, stress, toxins or trauma, it overheats and creates toxic byproducts. This leads to pain, redness and swelling as the blood vessels dilate. Cooling, alkalizing therapies reduce Pitta's sharp quality and relieve this irritation.

General tips for reducing inflammation include avoiding Pitta-aggravating foods like tomatoes, eggplants, chilies, vinegar, fermented foods and sour citrus. Favor sweet, bitter and astringent foods that balance Pitta. Manage stress through yoga and meditation. Stay well hydrated, especially with anti-inflammatory green tea. Apply cool compresses to inflamed areas. Take probiotics to improve gut health and immunity.

Turmeric contains the potent anti-inflammatory compound curcumin. Take 400-600mg turmeric supplements 1-2x daily. Cook with fresh or powdered turmeric. Combine with black pepper to increase absorption.

A Comprehensive Journey into Ayurvedic Healing

Turmeric relieves joint pain, counters excess Pitta and clears toxins. It can be used both acutely and long-term.

Ginger is another rhizome that reduces inflammation. It inhibits production of inflammatory prostaglandins. Have ginger tea daily, use it in cooking or take supplements. Apply diluted ginger oil topically with massage. Ginger calms Pitta, aids digestion and improves circulation. It offers broad anti-inflammatory effects.

Omega-3 fatty acids like those in fish oil and flax seeds inhibit inflammatory mediators. They provide building blocks for anti-inflammatory hormones. Take 1-2 grams daily of fish, flax or algal oil. Include oily fish and chia/flax seeds in your diet. Omega-3s lubricate joints, calm Pitta and aid cognition.

Ashwagandha is an adaptogenic Ayurvedic herb that regulates inflammatory pathways. Take 500mg standardized extract 1-2x daily. It contains withanolides that suppress cytokine production. Ashwagandha reduces joint pain, counters stress and stabilizes moods. It rejuvenates tissues and balances hormones.

The Ayurvedic formula Triphala is composed of three antioxidant fruits that reduce inflammation. Take 1/4 to 1 teaspoon of powder or tablets nightly. Triphala detoxifies the GI tract, scrapes away ama and minimizes free radical damage. Its anti-inflammatory benefits relieve joint pain.

Bromelain and papain are anti-inflammatory enzymes found in pineapple and papaya. Eating fresh fruit daily aids their absorption. Alternatively take 400-500mg bromelain supplement between meals. These protein-digesting enzymes reduce prostaglandin production and alleviate swelling.

Boswellia serrata contains boswellic acids that prevent inflammatory leukotrienes formation. Take 400-900mg daily. The resin relieves joint pain and counters autoimmune diseases driven by inflammation. Boswellia is traditionally used to treat inflammatory disorders. It reduces edema and immobility.Willow bark contains salicin which the body converts to salicylic acid, the pain-relieving component of aspirin. Take 500-1000mg capsules 3 times daily with food. Willow bark reduces inflammation, joint pain and fevers without irritating the stomach. Use it instead of aspirin long-term.

Cayenne and other warming spices like ginger, cinnamon and black pepper relieve pain by depleting nerve cell's substance P which communicates pain signals. Apply capsaicin cream containing cayenne topically or take 25,000-50,000 Scoville units cayenne capsules.

Cilantro, fennel and coriander seeds promote detoxification in the body to reduce inflammatory byproducts of metabolism. Use liberally in cooking or take 1-2 teaspoons powdered in capsules daily. These carminative seeds aid digestion and elimination as well.

Include antioxidant-rich fruits and vegetables like berries, pomegranates, dark leafy greens, and cruciferous vegetables in your diet. Their anti-inflammatory phytonutrients help prevent and relieve pain and swelling long-term by reducing free radical damage.

Use ice packs or cold compresses on inflamed areas to constrict blood vessels and reduce swelling. Apply for 10-15 minutes several times a day. Contrast baths alternating hot and cold also improve circulation. Apply soothing aloe vera gel.

Eliminate inflammatory foods like fried foods, simple carbs, alcohol, dairy and food allergens. Limit red meat and transition to anti-inflammatory foods like fatty fish, leafy greens, healthy fats and spices. An anti-inflammatory diet is essential.

A Comprehensive Journey into Ayurvedic Healing

Daily yoga asanas like gentle forward bends, twists and hip openers encourage circulation in joints and tissues. Hold stretches for 1-2 minutes using props to relax muscles. Move slowly with mindfulness, avoiding pain. Yoga releases cytokines that drive inflammation.

Cultivate compassion, forgiveness and equanimity through spiritual practices. Let go of anger and resentment. Unresolved emotions cause conflict and disturb sympathetic function. Approach challenges with mindfulness. Practice non-reaction. Reduce inflammatory mental states.

Massaging affected areas with medicated herbal oils provides analgesic effects. Use soothing oils like coconut, brahmi, sunflower and mustard oil. Add a few drops of peppermint, eucalyptus or wintergreen essential oil. Massage inflamed joints gently.

Soak in an Epsom salt bath to reduce swelling and pain. Magnesium absorbs through the skin to relax muscles and buffer inflammatory chemicals. Soothe aches after exercise this way. Avoid prolonged hot baths which tax the heart.

As with any condition, individualized Ayurvedic care from a practitioner may be needed for lasting results. Receive herb and diet guidance based on your unique constitution, imbalances and symptoms. Follow Panchakarma treatments to purify deep toxins. Then continue rejuvenative therapies at home.

8.3 Treatments for Anxiety and Insomnia

Ayurveda offers natural approaches to calm restless Vata, soothe fiery Pitta and stimulate dull Kapha to balance mind and body for restful sleep. By managing the doshas, lifestyle, diet and environment, Ayurvedic therapies relieve anxiety, reduce excess mental stimulation and establish regular sleep rhythms.

Healthy sleep emerges from routine. Maintain a consistent sleep schedule, waking and sleeping at the same times daily. This synchronizes the body's inner clock or Vata dosha which regulates our circadian rhythms. Set a calming mood during the hours leading up to bedtime. Dim the lights, engage in soothing activities and avoid overstimulation.

Abhyanga, or Ayurvedic oil massage before bed, deeply relaxes the nervous system. Choose sesame, almond or coconut oil. Apply oil over the entire body using long, firm strokes. Massage the head, ears and feet which contain many pacifying marma points. Then take a warm bath or shower to allow the oil to penetrate.

In the evening, have a light warm meal of porridge, soup or khichari with spices like cumin, fennel, ginger and turmeric which balance Vata. Avoid cold, raw foods at night which disrupt sleep. Drink a cup of warm milk with turmeric, cinnamon and cardamom or bedtime tea with herbs like chamomile, passionflower and ashwagandha.

Practice calming yoga poses before bed like forward bends, child's pose and supported backbends. Relaxing pranayama like alternate nostril breathing induces tranquility. Release any emotional turmoil through journaling. Expressing feelings prevents internalization.

Apply sesame oil to the soles of the feet and crown of the head before bed. Massaging these marma points deeply calms Vata and Pitta, promoting sound sleep. Use a little lavender or chamomile essential oil for added relaxation.

Have the head of your bed face east to align with the sun's energy. Keep the mattress firm and bedroom cool. Use soft red, white and black bedding which are moonlight colors. Burn a little frankincense resin to purify the space. Maintain quiet, clean, comfortable bedrooms.

Take 500-1000mg of Brahmi daily to soothe the nervous system and release emotional tension. Brahmi is renowned for bestowing restful sleep and steadying the mind from excessive thinking. It relieves anxiety, mental fatigue and racing thoughts at bedtime.

Practice relaxing yoga nidra (yogic sleep) for 20-30 minutes upon going to bed. Lie on your back and follow a guided meditation that takes you through deep relaxation of each body part. Allow yourself to sink into a receptive mode. Then continue into sleep.

If you can't fall asleep within 20 minutes, get up and try an activity like light reading or listening to soft music. Avoid stimulating television and phones. Then return to bed when sleepy. Lying awake in bed builds frustration which disturbs sleep further.

Enjoy a warm, sesame oil-infused foot massage before bed. Marma points on the soles release melatonin and serotonin while balancing Vata in the nervous system. Applying oil to the head and feet induces deep tranquility and sound sleep.Take 300-600mg of standardized ashwagandha root extract daily to reduce excess Vata and anxiety. Ashwagandha relieves stress, calms the mind and promotes restorative sleep. It nourishes the nervous system and counters hyperarousal. Ashwagandha can be used long term without grogginess.

Diffuse calming essential oils like lavender, marjoram, sandalwood, neroli or clary sage at bedtime. Inhaling their aroma soothes the nervous system and mind. Add several drops to your pillowcase. Mix with a carrier oil and massage feet, neck and temples.

Practice alternate nostril breathing, nadi shodhana, in the evening - inhaling and exhaling slowly through left then right nostrils. This pranayama balances sympathetic and parasympathetic nervous systems to induce tranquility. End your practice by holding both nostrils closed and suspended for retention.

Limit exposure to electronics and screens an hour before bed as the blue light suppresses melatonin production. Wear amber tinted glasses to block blue light wavelengths if using devices at night. Darkness signals the pineal gland to release melatonin which regulates sleep.

Establish a soothing pre-bed ritual like journaling feelings, light stretching, energetic self-massage, brewing sleepytime tea. Activities to transition the mind from thinking into parasympathetic rest and renewal. Let go of the day's concerns.

Take magnesium supplements before bed as magnesium relaxes muscles, counters anxiety and regulates nervous system activity. Magnesium bisglycinate, citrate or glycinate are well-absorbed forms. Calcium and magnesium have a see-saw relationship so maintain proper balance.

Set a regular meditation practice ideally morning and evening. Meditating before bed quiets mental turbulence that interferes with sleep. Observe the space between your thoughts. Let go of ruminating thoughts through passive detachment. Empty the mind into restful awareness.

Avoid stimulating sensory input before bed like exciting television shows, news or arguments. Keep conversation light and upbeat. Read spiritual literature or fiction. Dim the home's lights and sounds to ease into sleep. Maintain your sleep sanctuary.

Practice mindful living during the day - being present for each activity without worrying about the future or ruminating about the past. Train your mind to stay focused in the now for restful sleep. Meditate on the current moment.

Seek counsel to resolve emotional conflicts which may underlie insomnia. Repressed trauma, grief and anger disrupt deep sleep. Talking through issues brings insight and completion. Follow mind-body therapies. Healing the psyche brings peace.

By skillfully managing stimuli, diet, herbal support and inner awareness during the day and evening, you can encourage balanced, restful sleep. However, consult an Ayurvedic practitioner for personalized guidance based on your unique imbalances and constitution. Lasting success treating insomnia requires an individualized approach addressing root causes. With nature's wisdom, you'll dissolve anxiety and rest deeply.

8.4 Caring for Skin, Hair and Teeth

Ayurveda offers natural approaches to skin care that cleanse, nourish and rejuvenate the skin while balancing the doshas. Proper diet, herbal oils, detox routines and lifestyle factors contribute to a clear, youthful complexion.

The state of our skin mirrors our inner health. Diet and digestion issues, stress, hormonal changes and toxin accumulation often manifest as skin imbalances. Pitta governs the skin, so fiery conditions like acne, rashes and premature aging signify excess internal heat. Cooling Pitta through diet and herbs clears the complexion.

For Vata skin that is dry, thin and rough, the key is nourishing and moisturizing. Use soothing oils for massage and hydrating creams. Favor sweet, salty and sour foods. Micronutrients like zinc, vitamin E and vitamin A lubricate dry skin. Avoiding excessive wind, cold and sun preserves moisture.

Kapha skin tends to be oily and prone to congestion. Stimulating massage and astringent herbs help decongest. Dry brushing improves circulation and toxin removal. Eat light, warm, spicy foods to increase metabolic fire. Bacterial overgrowth contributes to acne - take probiotics. Reduce oiliness with cleansing grains like barley.

The Ayurvedic herbal formula Triphala tones and detoxifies the skin. Its combination of amalaki, bibhitaki and haritaki removes impurities and congestion. Take 1/4 tsp with warm water at night, or make into a paste with water and apply topically as a face mask. Rinse after 10 minutes.

Manjistha, or Indian madder root, purifies the blood and lymphatics to clear skin conditions. Take 300mg daily, or add manjistha powder to face masks. It reduces redness, inflammation, and breakouts by detoxifying tissue layers underneath the skin. Manjistha improves lustre and glow.

Neem leaf and its oil exhibit antibacterial, antiviral and anti-inflammatory properties to treat acne and irritation. Apply diluted neem oil to acne spots. Consume neem tablets or use neem powder in face masks to cleanse deeply. Neem's bitter taste clears heat as well.

The Ayurvedic herb Guduchi brightens and rejuvenates the skin through its antioxidant effects. Guduchi also balances Pitta and removes toxins that damage the skin. Consume guduchi powder or capsules daily. Add it to face masks or use it as a medicinal skin toner. Guduchi improves collagen production.

A paste made from chickpea or urad dahl and turmeric makes an effective exfoliant to remove dead skin cells and rejuvenate the skin. The antioxidants in turmeric heal the underlying skin while gentle abrasion from the legumes smoothes and brightens. Rinse the paste thoroughly after rubbing skin in circles.

Retinoids promote skin turnover for a radiant complexion. Food sources like carrots, sweet potatoes, spinach, chard and apricots contain beta carotene which forms vitamin A. Take 25,000 IU vitamin A supplements daily, not to exceed 100,000 IU. Vitamin A enables new skin cell generation.

Drink at least 64 ounces of water daily to hydrate the skin from within. Eat juicy fruits and vegetables with a high liquid content. Oil massage and indirect steam from boiled water also supply moisture. Avoid excess sun and wind exposure which dehydrate delicate facial skin. Adequate hydration gives a healthy glow.Getting adequate rest maintains youthful skin. Sleep allows tissue regeneration, repair and detoxification. Sleep deficiency causes dark under eye circles, dull complexion and wrinkles. Follow an early, regular sleep schedule and natural ritual to encourage sound beauty sleep.

Managing stress through yoga, meditation and life balance prevents stress hormones from inflaming and aging the skin. Anxious, hurried energy leads to wrinkles and blemishes. Cultivate equanimity and self-acceptance to avoid perfectionistic, critical mental states.

Certain lifestyle factors damage the skin like excessive sun exposure, smoking, pollution and lack of exercise. Avoid overexposure to sun and tanning beds. Apply non-toxic sunscreen when outdoors. Anti-oxidant rich foods protect against free radicals from poor lifestyle habits.

For soft, glowing skin, perform abhyanga daily - Ayurvedic warm oil self-massage. Use organic, cold-pressed oils like sesame, coconut, almond or safflower. Massage the entire body before bathing to allow oils to penetrate skin. This deeply hydrates and rejuvenates.

Spring is the season to do therapeutic fasting and cleansing routines to detoxify the body and clear the complexion. Consult an Ayurvedic practitioner about appropriate Panchakarma purification treatments for your constitution. Fasting cleanses ama while oleation smoothes and softens the skin.

Assure adequate protein intake through diet - eggs, legumes, dairy products, nuts and lean meats supply amino acids for building healthy dermal tissue. Deficiency causes dryness and thinning. Beans and rice together make a complete protein. Nourish your skin from within through diet.

Relieve constipation and maintain 2-3 bowel movements daily to remove toxins through the GI tract. Triphala is excellent before bed. Drink plenty of fluids and eat fiber-rich fruits and vegetables. Proper daily elimination prevents toxin backlog that damages skin.

Steaming the face over a pot of boiled herb water softens and hydrates the skin while drawing out impurities. Add skin-friendly herbs like calendula, comfrey, rose petals or lavender. Then rinse your face with cool water to close pores. Steam 2-3x weekly for radiant skin.

For pimples and acne, apply pure tea tree essential oil diluted with a carrier oil like coconut oil. Its anti-viral, antibacterial action clears pores and speeds healing without drying the skin. Dab on blemishes twice daily after cleansing. Tea tree oil balances all three doshas.

Include bioflavonoid-rich foods in your diet like berries, citrus fruits, green leafy vegetables, beans and onions. Bioflavonoids protect the skin from sun damage and improve collagen production. They have potent anti-oxidant, anti-inflammatory benefits for skin cells. Aim for 1-2 servings of foods rich in bioflavonoids daily.

Consult an Ayurvedic practitioner for lasting, holistic results. Receive customized guidance for diet, herbs, lifestyle, detoxification and internal balance of doshas. Constitutional remedies address the root causes of skin imbalances for authentic healing. Combine outer care with inner transformation through Ayurveda's complete wisdom.

8.5 Gynecological Care

Ayurveda offers natural ways to support women's health during menstruation, fertility, pregnancy and menopause. Balancing hormones, herbs, yoga, massage and dietary changes help alleviate common symptoms while nurturing optimal wellness.

The menstrual cycle Vata, Pitta and Kapha phases govern menstruation. Premenstrually Kapha accumulates, stimulating Pitta at menses which moves Vata downward to shed the uterine lining. Imbalances in the doshas cause associated symptoms. Aligning with the body's rhythms prevents problems.

Yoga asanas like Bound Angle, Bridge, Child's pose and standing poses encourage downward flow during menses. Pranayama balances the solar and lunar energetic currents. Inverted postures calm excessive flow. Avoid strong backbends which open the womb. Gentle movement stabilizes cycles.

Castor oil packs over the lower abdomen help relax uterine muscles to ease cramps and pain. Apply castor oil packs during menses when Apana Vata is active. The oil's heating quality relaxes spasms while supporting circulation. Massaging with castor oil also relieves pain.

Healthy fats help mitigate PMS symptoms like mood swings which arise from hormone changes. Consume plenty of omega-3 foods like walnuts, chia seeds and fatty fish. Avoid hormone-disrupting trans fats from fried and processed foods. Reduce Pitta-aggravating salts, spices and alcohol.

Golden milk combines anti-inflammatory turmeric with nourishing dairy to balance hormones and soothe the system premenstrually. Add 1/2 teaspoon turmeric to heated milk with cinnamon, cardamom, saffron and honey. Turmeric's manganese regulates hormones while dairy pacifies Vata and Pitta.

Chasteberry fruit balances hormones by supporting pituitary gland function. Take 400-900mg daily, beginning after menses and continuing until menstruation starts. Chasteberry regulates ovulation, moderates

PMS symptoms and stabilizes erratic cycles. Introduce slowly over 3 months for best results.

Ayurvedic botanicals like Shatavari, Ashoka bark and Lodhra promote reproductive health. Shatavari nourishes female organs and enhances fertility. Ashoka improves uterine circulation. Lodhra calms Pitta in the pelvis. Many classical Ayurvedic formulas combine these with dashamoola herbs. Ask your practitioner for guidance.

For heavy bleeding, take 500-1000mg of lady's mantle herb daily. Its astringent tannins contract tissues. Bolster weakened uterine muscles prone to flooding. Drink raspberry leaf tea to tone the uterus. Apply a castor oil pack over the womb to ease spasms and congestion triggering excess flow.

A kitchari cleanse during onset of menses gives the body rest from digesting heavier foods while providing nourishment. The warming spices ginger, cumin and fenugreek enhance agni gently during menses. Light foods allow the body's energy to cleanse rather than digest. Rest more during this monthly ritual.

Schedule bodywork before and during menses when body and emotions need nurturing most. Receive therapeutic massage, energy balancing or craniosacral therapy. Express emotions and tender feelings through counseling or support groups. Honor inner sensitivity rather than suppressing it.The transition of menopause again highlights balancing Vata for stability. Stress-reducing self-care minimizes hot flashes, heart palpitations and insomnia from Vata aggravation. Yoga, meditation, massage and spending time in nature ease this passage. Vata-pacifying foods, herbs and oils support equilibrium.

For fertility, tone the female reproductive system with herbs like Shatavari. It nourishes the ovum while supporting healthy mucus secretions. Ashwagandha balances hormones to improve ovulation and uterine health. Take 1-2 capsules of each herb daily for 3-6 months alongside dietary adjustments.

Ginger-ashwagandha tea enhances fertility by increasing circulation to the pelvis and regulating menstrual cycles. Simmer 1/2 teaspoon powdered ginger and 1/2 teaspoon ashwagandha with 1 cup milk and 1 teaspoon ghee. Sweeten with raw honey. Have daily to harmonize hormone function.

The traditional Ayurvedic preparatory procedure Purvakarma optimizes chances of conception. Herbal cleansing, meditation, yoga and Pancha Karma open blocked energy channels and balance hormones. Purvakarma harmonizes bodily rhythms and creates a nurturing inner ecosystem to welcome pregnancy.

Eating adequate good quality fats is vital for hormone balance. Focus on omega-3 fatty acids which reduce inflammation. Include anti-oxidant rich olives, avocados, nuts, seeds and their oils. Avoid rancid, damaged or hydrogenated fats. Seek healthy fats at each meal for optimal hormonal flow.

Manage lifestyle stress through routines, boundaries and delegating obligations nonessential to your wellbeing. Make time for hobbies, friends, music, movement and nature. Adrenal exhaustion from overwork inhibits fertility. Bring joy and leisure into daily life to unwind worry.

The traditional Ayurvedic formulation Phala Ghritam taken postpartum replenishes vital nutrients lost during pregnancy and delivery. It contains almond oil and key herbs like ashwagandha, vidarikanda and shatavari. Take 1-2 teaspoons twice daily with warm milk as an herbal tonic.

New mothers need adequate rest and help with responsibilities. Observe traditional Ayurvedic rest period for recovery after birth. Receive massage, warm baths, nurturing foods like ghee rice pudding and emotional support. This essential ritual honors a new mother's sensitive transition.

Overall, revitalizing self-care sustains women through menstrual cycles, fertility, pregnancy, postpartum and menopause. Herbs, diet, massage, emotional support, spiritual nourishment and Ayurvedic cleansing establish optimal wellbeing. Partner with a practitioner for customized guidance. Thrive by respecting the goddess within!

8.6 Pediatric Health and Wellness

Ayurveda offers gentle, natural therapies to support children's health, development and wellbeing. Keeping the doshas balanced through diet, herbs, yoga and massage maximizes vitality during each phase of growth. Addressing issues early prevents bigger problems later.

Setting regular daily routines provides stability as active Vata dosha predominates in childhood. Consistent mealtimes, naps, play and sleep times give comfort. Make mornings slow and relaxed - avoid the frantic rush typical of school days. Check with your Ayurvedic practitioner about age-appropriate routines.

Soothe common Vata imbalances like gas, constipation or anxiety gently through massage. Abhyanga with soothing oils like coconut calms and integrates the nervous system. Oil massage before bedtime prevents insomnia. Gently knead the belly to relieve gas pain. Yoga postures calm hyperactivity.

Kapha accumulates naturally in childhood, so providing energetic play opportunities counteracts inertia. Avoid too much screen time or repetitive activities. Alternate active play outdoors with quieter indoor play. Help Kapha kids transition flexibly between stimulating activities and rest.

Keep the home environment simple, calm and orderly to prevent sensory overload for impressionable Vata. Play soothing nature sounds, use soft lighting, minimize clutter and keep a predictable schedule. Prepare meals with love - family dinner prevents Vata isolation.

As Pitta energy emerges after age six approximately, discourage competition and teach equanimity. Provide ways to constructively channel intensity like sports or creative arts. Teach self-acceptance, empathy and adapting to changes versus rigid perfectionism.

Incorporate yoga poses and breathing practices daily to reduce stress hormones and balance the nervous system. Restorative poses like a child's pose calm Vata. Cooling forward folds and moon salutations balance rising Pitta. Kapha benefits from energizing sequences, sun salutes and backbends.

Breastfeeding provides essential nutrition and antibodies that support immunity in the vulnerable first year. The mother's diet should favor warm, unctuous foods to increase breast milk while soothing Vata in the baby. Gradually introduce wholesome solid foods after 6 months per pediatric Ayurvedic guidance.

As digestive strength increases after a year, add mild spices like cumin, fennel and ginger to aid food assimilation. Well-cooked whole grains, proteins and cooked vegetables nourish growing bodies. Introduce more Kapha and Pitta balancing foods gradually while monitoring reactions.

At puberty's onset, establish routines to balance hormonal changes and ease emotional ups and downs. Warm oil massage, yoga and meditation help integrate new energy flows. Guide teens in creative expression, time in nature and contribution to community. Allow space for inner growth.

For indigestion, colic, diarrhea or constipation try fennel tea, ginger water or mint water sweetened lightly with raw honey. 1/2 to 1 teaspoon triphala powder steeped overnight in a cup of hot water also gently relieves constipation and cleanses the GI tract. Consult your Ayurvedic pediatrician. Ayurveda offers a holistic approach to caring for children's health and promoting their overall wellbeing. As we've explored, the ancient wisdom of Ayurveda emphasizes balance as the key to optimal health. This principle applies just as much to growing kids as it does to adults. In Ayurvedic pediatrics, treatments are carefully tailored to each child's unique constitution and aimed at gently bringing their doshas back into harmony.

For infants and young children especially, maintaining regular daily and seasonal routines is profoundly important. Following a consistent schedule of sleeping, feeding, bathing, playing and learning activities nurtures healthy physical, emotional and mental development. Traditionally, Ayurvedic physicians emphasized that children thrive when provided warmth, touch, affection and attention from caring parents and elders. Showing love through hugging, singing, story-telling, massage and co-sleeping enables kids to feel safe and connected.

As children grow, their daily routines expand to include more robust dinacharya self-care practices. Teaching techniques like oil pulling, tongue scraping and nasal irrigation to pre-teens boosts immunity and prevents disease. Ayurveda also recognizes that older kids need plenty of free outdoor play time and light physical activity to burn their natural Kapha energy. Organized sports can be excellent, but shouldn't dominate a child's schedule. Making study time active by reciting lessons aloud or writing them out by hand enhances learning.

A Comprehensive Journey into Ayurvedic Healing

Kids and teens will benefit greatly from a simplified version of the Ayurvedic seasonal eating plan. In fall and winter, warm nourishing foods like stews, soups and porridges balance Vata. Come spring, lighter fare including sprouts, berries and leafy greens pacify Kapha. In summer's heat, cool Pitta with juicy fruits, cucumbers and mint. Minimizing cold, heavy and overly processed items keeps digestion strong. While allowing some treats, provide ample fresh whole foods. Understanding children's constitutional tendencies helps customize their diets further.

Herbal remedies can also gently support children's health. Many Ayurvedic herbs like fennel, cardamom, chamomile and gotu kola are safe and effective for kids when used judiciously. Syrups or honey are often used to administer child-friendly formulas that address common pediatric issues like colic, congestion, coughs, diarrhea, fever and teething discomfort. Always consult an Ayurvedic practitioner specialized in pediatrics before giving herbs to babies or children.

Childhood is also the time to lay crucial foundations for lifelong mental and emotional wellbeing. Ayurveda recognizes that kids are especially sensitive and absorbent, so positive behavioral modeling is vital. Creating a nurturing, ethical and spiritual home environment helps instill sattvic qualities like empathy, honesty and self-discipline. Exposure to nature, arts, music and community service also fosters healthy development.

Parents can utilize Ayurveda's wisdom on balancing Vata, Pitta and Kapha personality traits when troubleshooting their child's behavioral problems or struggles. Anxious and sensitive Vata types thrive on calming, regularity and reassurance. Intense, perfectionistic Pitta kids benefit from cooling routines and help channel their drive constructively. Slow-moving Kapha children need energetic stimulation and variety to stay focused. With care and conscious parenting, children grow into balanced, purposeful teens and adults.

As in adults, obesity and diabetes have become increasingly prevalent in children, which Ayurveda attributes to rampant lifestyle imbalances. Gentle detoxification through massage, hydration and an alkaline-favoring diet helps restore leaner body weight and metabolic function. Yoga poses like triangles, backbends and lunges integrated into play build strength. Pranayama breathing practices calm the mind and nervous system. Guided meditation and contemplative activities relieve stress. For adolescents facing more serious mood disorders or trauma, Ayurvedic psychology offers supportive counseling and rasayanas to nourish the mind.

Throughout childhood and adolescence, getting adequate sound sleep is critical to kids' growth, learning, immunity and hormone regulation. Starting a regular evening wind-down routine helps signal rest. Keeping televisions and digital devices out of bedrooms minimizes overstimulating "blue light." Massaging the scalp and feet with soothing oils and primes sleep. Herbs like brahmi, jatamansi, passionflower and valerian relax the nervous system. Establishing healthy nocturnal sleep in youth prevents later insomnia and burn-out.

When acute illnesses arise, Ayurvedic therapies can quickly relieve symptoms and aid recovery alongside any needed conventional treatments. At the first sign of infection, immune-bolstering formulas with tulsi, ginger, garlic and turmeric may help prevent full progression. Digestive upsets respond well to carminative herbs like cumin, fennel, coriander and cardamom. Honey and licorice root soothe sore throats and coughs. Peppermint, fennel and ginger teas reduce fever by clearing heat. Mild purgatives can short-circuit constipation while avoiding gut-irritating laxatives. Guided imagery, aromatherapy, Epsom salt baths and massage soothe body aches.

Every child's path to vibrant health is unique. Yet by leveraging Ayurveda's timeless wisdom on nurturing mind-body balance throughout childhood, parents have a powerful ally. With much love and consciousness, children can be raised to embody their fullest potential.

Dr. Emily L. Lad

Closing Remarks:

Our journey through this book exploring the profound wisdom of Ayurveda is drawing to a close. Yet in many ways, your journey with Ayurveda is just beginning.

Hopefully these pages have illuminated how profoundly Ayurveda's holistic principles apply to every facet of health and wellbeing. Far more than just a system of medicine, Ayurveda offers complete guidance on living in harmony with nature's rhythms and your unique mind-body constitution. Its insights on nutrition, routines, detoxification, herbalism, yoga and the mental landscape provide an intricate roadmap to optimal vitality and self-realization.

While absorbing this wealth of information, you've probably recognized many areas where your lifestyle could better support balance. Don't feel daunted by how much dietary fine-tuning, daily discipline or discernment adopting Ayurveda may require initially. Start with small steps like eating warmer, lighter foods, establishing a calming nightly routine, meditating for a few minutes daily or taking triphala to improve digestion. Add additional practices gradually as they feel nourishing. Be patient with yourself as old habits transform.

Commit to this path of svasthya - true health - not out of anxiety about sickness, but from a deep desire for enlightened living. Know that anything undertaken with pure intention has the power to heal and uplift you. The more you listen to your body's wisdom through Ayurveda's lens, the more your external routines will align with your inner needs. Progress will come through sustained practice.

While this book offers a comprehensive introduction, Ayurveda's sophisticated treatments and nuanced diagnostics require expert guidance. I encourage you to consult reputable Ayurvedic practitioners at health centers or colleges for personalized advice, especially when handling chronic or complex imbalances. Don't view Ayurveda and modern medicine as mutually exclusive, but complementary sciences to integrate for complete care.

I hope you will continue expanding your Ayurvedic knowledge through further reading, training, cooking classes and even trips to India. But what matters most is weaving Ayurveda's principles into your daily life. Maintaining awareness around how different foods, activities and seasons affect your doshas is a lifelong practice. Let Ayurveda slip into your habits through intention and repetition, like water smoothing a stone. Before long, you'll think, act and live from an Ayurvedic state of balance effortlessly.

While this book covered many key aspects of Ayurveda, entire tomes could be written on its vast teachings. I encourage you to never stop learning, questioning or growing your understanding. Yet don't make intellectual study a substitute for direct experience. The ultimate authority on what restores your unique state of prakriti lies within you. Listen to your heart.

I hope your journey with Ayurveda is filled with luminous health, joyful self-discovery, and conscious living. May you transform not just your own life, but uplift those around you by sharing Ayurveda's light. The world needs Ayurveda's wisdom now more than ever. Let us bring forth health, compassion and balance for all beings.

www.ingramcontent.com/pod-product-compliance
Lightning Source LLC
Chambersburg PA
CBHW051822150726
47998CB00001B/254